Dignity and Grace

Dignity and Grace

Wisdom for Caregivers and Those Living with Dementia

Janet L. Ramsey

DIGNITY AND GRACE
Wisdom for Caregivers and Those Living with Dementia

Copyright © 2018 Fortress Press. All rights reserved. Except for brief
quotations in critical articles or reviews, no part of this book may be
reproduced in any manner without prior written permission from
the publisher. Email copyright@1517.media or write to Permissions,
Fortress Press, PO Box 1209, Minneapolis, MN 55440-1209.

All biblical references in this book come from the New Revised
Standard Version, unless otherwise noted.

Cover and interior design: Rob Dewey
Typesetting: PerfecType, Nashville, TN

Print ISBN: 978-1-5064-3178-9
eBook ISBN: 978-1-5064-3422-3

The paper used in this publication meets the minimum
requirements of American National Standard for Information
Sciences — Permanence of Paper for Printed Library Materials,
ANSI Z329.48-1984.

Manufactured in the U.S.A.

For my children, Jason, Benjamin, Leigh, Katherine, and Brian—
with all my love.

Contents

Series Preface

MY MOST sincere wish is that the Living with Hope series will offer comfort, wisdom—and hope—to individuals facing life's most common and intimate challenges. Books in the series tackle complex problems such as addiction, parenting, unemployment, pregnancy loss, serious illness, trauma, and grief and encourage individuals, their families, and those who care for them. The series is bound together by a common message for those who are dealing with significant issues: you are not alone. There is hope.

This series offers first-person perspectives and insights from authors who know personally what it is like to face these struggles. As companions and guides, series contributors share personal experiences, offer valuable research from trusted experts, and suggest questions to help readers process their own responses and explore possible next steps. With empathy and honesty, these accessible volumes reassure individuals they are not alone in their pain, fear, or confusion.

The series is also a valuable resource for pastoral and spiritual care providers in faith-based settings. Parish pastors, lay ministers, chaplains, counselors, and other staff and volunteers can draw on these volumes to offer skilled and compassionate guidance to individuals in need of hope.

Each title in this series is offered with prayer for the reader's journey—one of discovery, further challenges, and transformation. You are not alone. There is hope.

Beth Ann Gaede, Series Editor

Titles in the Living with Hope Series

Nurturing Hope: Christian Pastoral Care in the Twenty-First Century (Lynne M. Baab)

Dignity and Grace: Wisdom for Caregivers and Those Living with Dementia (Janet L. Ramsey)

Jobs Lost, Faith Found: A Spiritual Resource for the Unemployed (Mary C. Lindberg)

They Don't Come with Instructions: Cries, Wisdom, and Hope for Parenting Children with Developmental Challenges (Hollie M. Holt-Woehl)

True Connection: Using the NAME IT Model to Heal Relationships (George Faller and Heather P. Wright)

Waiting for Good News: Living with Chronic and Serious Illness (Sally L. Wilke)

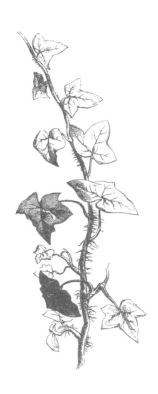

Acknowledgments

THIS BOOK depended on the gracious help and support of many people. First, I thank the caregivers who shared their stories with me, both those I interviewed specifically for this book and those who told me their stories over the years in my pastoral counseling office. You were my teachers; you are the experts who are responsible for any wisdom in these pages. Thanks also to those I counseled with memory impairments. Your courage is an inspiration to me.

Second, I thank my patient and talented editor at Fortress Press, Beth Gaede. I know that this book would be far different without your amazing help, and I will miss our almost daily chats. Thank you, thank you!

Thanks also to the pastors who introduced me to caregivers who accompany loved ones with impaired memories. Because of the need for confidentiality, I cannot name you, but please know how much I appreciate the time and energy you spent making these interviews possible.

I also thank my colleagues at Luther Seminary, particularly Rolf Jacobson, who taught me to love the psalms; Alan Padgett, who modeled how to talk about personal faith with authenticity; and Fred Gaiser, who understands so deeply that the intersection of faith and health is biblical. Special thanks to my colleague and friend Lois Malcolm, whose love of Paul Tillich and whose ability to articulate the deep structures of systematic theology have changed the way I think, forever.

Finally, I thank my husband, Joe Ramsey, for his love and support. You are my best friend and you make me laugh, every day.

Part One

Dignity

This Is Not What I Thought Would Happen Next: The Dementia Diagnosis

WHAT WAS the most important day of your life? Perhaps if someone asked you this question, you would answer by talking about the day you were baptized, the magical moment when you became a parent, or the proud time when you earned a promotion at work. But Kristin, sixty-nine, has a different event near the top of her list—the day her husband was diagnosed with dementia. "My life is divided into before and after. On that day, walking out of the doctor's office, I thought everything had suddenly come to an end," she says.

Today, Kristin has changed her perspective. I interviewed her five years after she heard this news, and she now speaks less dramatically about her situation. "Overall, my husband and I are coping with this illness [Parkinson's disease] and with the changes it brought. We even laugh together sometimes, believe it or not. It hasn't been easy. It's been the toughest thing we've ever gone through, but it isn't the end of the world either."

If you are a person who has been diagnosed with dementia yourself, or if you are a caregiver who is accompanying someone with this illness, you may find yourself on a journey that began much like Kristin's—with a sudden diagnosis and an acute sense of panic. On the other hand, your journey may have started gradually, as you realized more and more each day that there were changes in yourself, or in your partner or parent.

Whether sudden or gradual, the impact of a diagnosis of dementia tends to reorganize a family's entire life. Dementia is a "plot breaker"[1] with the power to disrupt the personal story lines of people who had other plans. "This is not what I thought would happen to me next in my life," Baroness Karen von Blixen tells her doctor in the movie *Out of Africa* after receiving a shocking diagnosis. How true this is for families experiencing dementia.

Kristin and her husband certainly did not expect this development. When they planned for their retirement years, they envisioned travel, volunteer work, and visits to the art museums they enjoy. Kristin told me that adjusting to dementia is an ongoing process. The sadness she feels in letting go of dreams continues, even as she adjusts to a new reality. These days she is always busy.

Sometimes her husband, Tom, can do things for himself, but other times he needs her help with simply putting on a robe. But the hands-on care is not what is most difficult for this couple. Since dementia became part of their lives, Kristin and Tom spend much of their time solving practical problems—getting to doctor's visits, monitoring the side effects of new medications, and working to prevent Tom from falling—again!

On the other hand, Kristin no longer sees dementia as "the end of the world." She has been able to move past her initial feelings of panic to gradual acceptance of their situation. She has learned to problem solve rather than catastrophize, and she is no longer paralyzed by anxiety. Kristin told me that she and Tom continue to have moments of real joy, as when the grandchildren visit, or moments when they can laugh together at "our crazy situation." "The other day we both stopped trying to get Tom's arm in the right sleeve of his sweater, and we laughed. What else can you do!"

Above all, Kristin has been grateful that her Christian faith and her spiritual community have been present in the days since the diagnosis—both the good days and those that are more difficult. "I couldn't have done this alone, without God's help!" she told

Whether sudden or gradual, the impact of a diagnosis of dementia tends to reorganize a family's entire life.

me. As a pastor, and as someone who has been focused on spiritual resiliency in my research and writing for many years, I was naturally pleased to hear her say this. But I was also well aware I must listen deeply to discern the pathways of faith she walked in her everyday life. Why did she feel now that she was going the wiser way?

There is certainly much in Kristin's new caregiving vocation that requires strength, as does her husband's new situation as he lives with memory impairment. They will need resiliency that has spiritual, social, and psychological dimensions. Her task began immediately, right after the diagnosis was given—trying to figure out exactly what all those clinical words meant.

Understanding the Language of Dementia

One of the first things caregivers like Kristin and their partners have to do when they hear a diagnosis of dementia is become acquainted with a whole world of confusing terminology. Many people, including caregivers themselves, have difficulties with the language used to describe persons with memory or other cognitive problems. What is the relationship between Alzheimer's disease and dementia in general? If someone is forgetful, does that mean they have dementia, or is that simply a normal part of old age?

All people experience cognitive changes as they age, including memory issues and slower response rates while doing tasks such as typing.[2] But when these problems begin to interfere with everyday life, it is time to visit a family physician or a geriatric assessment clinic. Forgotten appointments, losing personal items repeatedly, increased irritability—these are only a few of the symptoms that send out a warning signal. Sometimes, family members find it difficult to take the step of visiting a doctor. Many people who are noticing memory changes find they prefer to deny what's going on rather than face the possibility of a diagnosis they don't want to hear. This can cost precious time, since strategies that can slow down dementia are delayed.

After hearing the word *dementia* from a professional, it is still easy to be unsure of exactly what it means. The easiest way to clear up this confusion is to think of the word *dementia* as an umbrella term under which fall separate illnesses that can all lead to problems with thinking and memory. A diagnosis of Alzheimer's disease, one form of dementia, can be especially difficult to hear since it is closely associated in our culture with the indignities of old age—with helplessness, confusion, and decline—and because it is a diagnosis without a cure. But as Kristin and Tom's story shows, many other illnesses can cause dementia, including Parkinson's disease, vascular disease, and Lewy body dementia. (I have provided a glossary of dementia terminology at the end of this book.) We need to become informed because, as I have found in numerous casual conversations, most people are unsure of these distinctions between the types of dementia and use them carelessly, confusing caregivers and their extended families. Kristin discovered this when she first shared Tom's diagnosis (of dementia related to Parkinson's) with her friends: "I didn't know he had Alzheimer's too!" one woman commented. Clearly, she was confusing the whole umbrella with one of the illnesses it covers.

But getting our medical language accurate is only the beginning of the challenges related to dementia language. One subtle but even more important problem arises when we exclusively use biomedical terminology to describe a human being. In a world of labels and diagnostic manuals, it is far too easy to objectify and dehumanize. If we thoughtlessly use medical terms and rely on labels, Tom, who has a lifetime of experience and a rich, complex personality, becomes, overnight, "the dementia patient with a chemical imbalance." His distress becomes "behavioral symptoms,"[3] and pharmacology seems the only solution. To think solely in terms of medicine is to take away much of what makes a human life valuable. This tendency decreases our motivation to listen carefully. And when we don't listen, we don't respond with sensitivity.

In order to retain respect for each unique person experiencing dementia, we need, first of all, to find ways to hear about and

In order to retain respect for each unique person experiencing dementia, we need, first of all, to find ways to hear about and understand the experience from their point of view.

understand the experience from their point of view. What does it feel like to find that we have forgotten where we live and are unsure of who we are?

Understanding the Experience of Dementia

A young woman working at a long-term care facility watches a tall, dignified old man walk down the hall. She doesn't fully understand what is going on with him but knows that he has some strange illness called dementia. He is clearly lost. When she asks him if she can help him find his room, he sighs and comments, "I'm a stranger in a strange land."

I was that young woman, more than fifty years ago, and these words were my first glimpse of the confusion that comes with dementia. I was working a summer job as a nurse's aide to help pay for my college tuition, and I was trying to find my own way through the confusing world of an intensive, long-term care facility. The words Mr. H spoke to me that day stayed with me through the years as I went on to a vocation in aging (gerontology)—including five years as a chaplain in a long-term care facility, a call as a pastor ministering to older members of my congregation, over twenty years as a marriage-and-family therapist specializing in aging, and finally as an academic professor/researcher/writer focused on gerontology. I also learned about this illness from being a long-distance caregiver to my own mother, whose last years included vascular dementia. Finally, during the months before writing this book, I learned from eight family and professional caregivers who told me stories about their lives as caregivers.

No one I met, however, has been more vivid than Mr. H in describing his experience—one of the many that I will explore throughout this book, because each person who must live with dementia is different. He was, indeed, feeling like a displaced person—like a stranger in a strange land. In many ways, I remain indebted to him and to his kind effort to share his experience with a naïve young woman who barely understood what he was saying.

I believe that all of us who are caregivers as well as those with impaired memories must learn as we listen to each other and allow the Holy Spirit to awaken our imagination and understanding, albeit in different ways. That principle will inform this book because, as with you who are experiencing life with dementia, I am learning still.

Who Are the Caregivers?

Like the term *dementia*, the word *caregiver* is used to refer to a variety of people in many different contexts. Some caregivers are family or close friends, living in the same home as the person experiencing dementia. They experience what has been called "the thirty-six-hour day," after a popular book of that title.[4] Others live close by the person with dementia but not in the same dwelling, perhaps because the person with dementia now needs the intensive care that a long-term care facility provides. Others live out of town or out of state and must help at a distance, often relying on local relatives to give daily care. As I discovered caring for my mother, long-distance caregivers experience a particular set of challenges, including guilt and worry.[5]

Still other caregivers are professionals who visit, counsel, and accompany as part of their full-time vocations. These caregivers are typically compassionate and sensitive people, and some of them have had years of experience with aging persons. They are the nurse's aides, physicians, nurses, social workers, chaplains, parish pastors, and psychologists. Their task is twofold—to care for a fragile patient but also to care for her partner, family members, and close friends. Many of these professionals become close to family caregivers and share with them important moments in the caregiving journey. Some also provide spontaneous spiritual care: the nurse's aide who was present when my mother-in-law was dying provided by far the most meaningful prayer that day.

Because we caregivers are such a diverse group, we bring a variety of resources and talents to our work. These resources and talents

I believe that all of us who are caregivers as well as those with impaired memories must learn as we listen to each other and allow the Holy Spirit to awaken our imagination and understanding, albeit in different ways.

determine, to a large extent, how we respond to various practical needs in our particular care setting. Our responses vary, however, not only from person to person but also across ethnic groups and cultures, and are specific to our historic period. Some caregivers have a wide and loving network of family and friends who are willing to help out, gladly providing emotional support and even hands-on respite care. This network may include neighbors, new friends in an Alzheimer's Association group, or old friends who are members of our congregation. Others feel alone or afraid to ask for help, in some cases because of unresolved family tensions but also perhaps because they were taught, as one woman I interviewed told me, to "be self-reliant at all costs."

Some caregivers have sufficient economic resources to pay for assistance with domestic chores and to purchase whatever equipment is needed, such as elevators and lifts for a family van. Others struggle to meet basic medical bills and must work full-time in addition to carrying out caregiving responsibilities. The depth and range of resources at a caregivers' disposal are important and can't be ignored in any discussion of caregiving.[6]

In addition to varied financial resources, time demands, and health status, we each bring to our caregiving responsibilities a unique combination of strengths and weakness, including our own mix of physical and emotional health. A surprising number of caregivers are coping with chronic medical conditions of their own and are deeply concerned about being able to stay healthy enough to continue as a caregiver. "I just worry about how long I'll be able to keep doing this," mentioned one woman I interviewed who struggles with hypertension.

But we are even more different psychologically. Those caregivers who have battled depression and/or anxiety all of their lives do not leave these challenges behind when they assume this role. Some caregivers use defense mechanisms, such as denial, that have been adequate for other situations in life but do not serve them well now, at a time when it is so important to be proactive. Some of us readily employ a problem-solving strategy when a crisis arises, while others feel undone by challenges great and small. Some of us are actors in our own private, unspoken story but others have an internal narrative in which they are the helpless victims of circumstance. Some caregivers never lose the capacity for hope, while others find themselves moving gradually toward despair. All of these people are part of the rich, complex mix of human beings who are caring for persons with dementia; all of them are the imperfect yet blessed ones who serve both God and our larger human family.

In addition, all of us have a relational history with the person who now needs our care, some untidy story of love, anger, forgiveness, resentments, bitterness, and empathy. This is the complex way we live together in our partnerships and families. The coming of dementia only highlights the immediate challenges within that ongoing relationship that both bring us together and keep us apart. The interviews I conducted before writing this book were a dramatic reminder of the truth that caregiving always occurs within the unique dynamics of a complex relationship and its intricate past. What an error it would be to visualize caregiving as one man or woman in isolation, giving care at the present moment. We need reminders, in our overly individualistic society, that we are bound together by an emotional and social web that we never fully understand.

Finally, we provide care within the imperfect, ever-changing cultural and historic moment. Life-span psychology has taught gerontologists, including this author, to bear in mind that all aspects of human development occur within a particular society, at a particular time. Our contemporary values impact our caregiving, often without our conscious awareness. For example, the unpaid nature of caregiving tends to devalue this work in our own and others' eyes. On the other hand, our culture provides technical resources that were not available to caregivers in the previous generations, such as social media and other resources on the internet, as well as promising medical research that can slow down dementias such as Alzheimer's disease. These challenges and advantages will be one of the dominant themes of this book, as I attempt to explore the experience of dementia for care partners as both a countercultural (i.e., Christian) enterprise and as a fortunate recipient of technological advances. These poles become especially important when we ask the question, "What do we hope for?"

What Might Our Hope Look Like?

During the open-ended, informal interviews I conducted just before writing this book, I always ended the conversations by asking, "What do you hope for?" I chose to leave this question general and did not specify what I meant by hope, in reference to either the person diagnosed with dementia or the caregiver. I was curious about where the person, who was kind enough to struggle with my question, would choose to focus—on her own needs, on those of the person with dementia, or even on our whole human family.

For some caregivers the response was quite specific and revealed an understandable longing for more time and opportunity to meet their basic personal needs. One woman, along with her husband, was caring for her mother-in-law with advanced Alzheimer's disease in their home. They took turns going out, attending church services, shopping, and so on. She cried a little as she told me, "I just hope to be able to go out to dinner with my husband now and then."

Another caregiver is presently making plans to move into a cottage that is part of a continuing-care facility. She anticipates getting some respite after the move and admitted she is hoping to take a cruise, perhaps with a close friend. Others focused on the care recipient, as the man who told me, "I just hope I can keep my mother out of a nursing home. Those places are dreadful!" Another hoped to be able to prevent more falls, and a different caregiver hoped for more help from her adult children.

I must confess to having some hope of my own as I conducted these interviews. I hoped that someone would respond by mentioning the hope beyond human hope, namely, the hope offered by our

What do you hope for?

spiritual faith. Then, finally, in one of the last interviews, I heard just that. Lorna had cared for her mother, who has Alzheimer's, for nine years at home before recently helping her move into assisted living. Articulate and open with me throughout the interview and thoughtful in her responses, she paused for several minutes after I asked this question. Then she spoke, "I hope for dignity and grace."

I was so moved by these words, and all that they evoked, that I chose to borrow them as the title for this book. Although others have spoken of dignity and grace in relationship to aging,[7] it is less likely that we would use these words to describe our hope for a severely impaired person with Alzheimer's disease living in a care facility. But I believe that Lorna spoke for all who are cognitively impaired, and those who give them care, when she so elegantly expressed her hope. To borrow the words of Mr. H, Lorna is acutely aware that her mother is traveling, like a new immigrant, into a strange, new land where everything and everyone is unknown. To navigate that terrain, she will need the two things we all need when we are lost and alone—dignity and grace. She also points to what she, as a caregiver, needs. Her task is often invisible and undervalued, disrespected in our economically driven society. And, like all of us, she needs the forgiving grace of God to move on after experiences of guilt and self-blame.

The words dignity and grace point to many aspects of caregiving. For example, caregivers hope that loved ones will always be treated with respect and seen as more than objects of care. They hope that nurse's aides will respond as promptly as possible to the bathroom needs of the one who is dependent on help. They hope that people will speak to their loved one in a non-patronizing, respectful tone of voice.

I believe dignity is also important for the caregiver herself, even though no one mentioned this. I was unhappy to discover the poor self-care of each person I interviewed, with one exception, Lorna, who said quite directly, "I'm good at asking for what I need." I heard stories of poor sleep, rare hours of respite, inadequate family/

friend care teams, and irregular physical exercise. Overall, the word *stress* echoed in my mind as I listened to the caregivers. While this is no surprise given the demands of their work, it is a real danger as well—for both caregiver and care recipient. How strange that our own needs are often last on our list. I fervently hope that this book will be both a reminder and a resource for improved dignity and self-care for those of you readers who are caregivers.

In addition to everyday, practical challenges for caregivers' health and well-being, there are also practical ramifications to the gift of grace. It takes a certain kind of patience to display repeated tolerance when a person with early stages of dementia repeats a story over and over, or asks the same question repeatedly. It takes grace to respond to the emotional content of words spoken by the cognitively impaired, rather than arguing with their incorrect factual content (we will explore communication techniques in more depth in chapter 2). And it takes grace to first confess our shortcomings as caregivers and then ask for God's forgiveness, thus setting us free to do the best that we can on any given day. It also takes grace for the person diagnosed with dementia to ask for help without irritability or shame—no small matter for those of us who are used to managing our own daily lives.

The following chapters of this book are my attempt to explore what dignity and grace have to do with living with dementia, either as a caregiver or as a person with memory impairment. I will also suggest how such a hope can be present amidst the exhausting, messy, and ambiguous work of giving care when dementia is present. My first "rule" is that there are no rules, at least not for how hope is present in each story. Each one of us has a different way of hearing Lorna's words and of appropriating them into our experience of dementia care. I encourage you to create your own story of dignity and grace as you read, perhaps editing it as you go. Hopefully by the conclusion of this book you will have arrived at a unique perspective of what hope looks like, both in your own life and in the life of the person you love and care for—if not now, then in the near future.

One final word about the book's title—the word "wisdom" in the subtitle refers primarily to the wisdom of the caregivers and persons living with dementia whom I interviewed, worked with as a counselor, and accompanied as a pastor. It also refers to biblical wisdom, particularly the wisdom of the Psalms. Finally, as my editor graciously reminds me, I have developed some level of wisdom myself through years of experience working with both caregivers and those with dementia, and from reflecting on those experiences with my students. Yet as I write this book, I am increasingly aware that we need, above all, the wisdom that God alone can give. "For the foolishness of God is wiser than human wisdom, and the weakness of God is stronger than human strength" (1 Cor 1:25).

My Theology of Caregiving

Lorna's words echoed for me the heart of Christian faith. First, I feel strongly that we have a dignity that no one can take away because it was given to us by a loving Creator God. Each of us is, first and foremost, a child of God. This core identity came before life handed us a diagnosis or a caregiving role. At baptism we were marked by the cross of Christ, forever. We cannot lose that mark of acceptance and worth even if, through dementia, we lose the ability to remember who and whose we are.

I believe, too, that we are given grace sufficient for all days and circumstances. This astonishing grace enables us to live with meaning and joy, even when we question our own standing with God or feel we have failed to follow, consistently, his will for our lives. We are forgiven; grace is ours—not because we can produce an income, participate in a witty conversation, or follow his commandments perfectly, but rather because the love of God was poured out for us in Christ's work on the cross.

As a Christian, I believe that God entered our world to teach us how to live, but also to replace scorekeeping with abundant forgiveness. I also take particular comfort in the message that, because of the Holy Spirit, we are not alone. I trust—or try to

At baptism we were marked by the cross of Christ, forever. We cannot lose that mark of acceptance and worth even if, through dementia, we lose the ability to remember who and whose we are.

trust—in the promise that whatever comes our way, we can dare to hope that grace will abound. We have a story to hold on to that I treasure: God's word tells us of Jesus—of his gentle healing, of the radical new values he preached, rejecting power and money as the basis for worth.

And I trust that grace will abound because we have a Savior who died in solidarity with our suffering. The great mystery of our faith is that, somehow, all our wounds are now part of Christ's wounds. When I wonder what has become of the personal suffering and brokenness of those I care for, I have a place to focus—namely, on the broken body of Christ. Paradoxically, it is on the cross of shame that dignity and grace are perfectly visible.

And so, I'm with Lorna. I hope that dignity and grace may be extended to me and to those I love in this life, whatever our cognitive status. I am grateful that these spiritual gifts are promised to us and made certain for all our unknown tomorrows. This includes the day we make our final goodbyes to those we love. Meanwhile, I strive to lean into the dignity and grace that are already mine. For although God provides all that I will ever need, it is up to me—to us all—to claim those gifts and to incorporate them into whatever vocation we choose (or that chooses us). This process of weaving God's gifts into our vocational lives is, of course, not a onetime event; it requires a lifetime of discipleship. I call the fruit of this labor *spiritual resiliency*.

Honesty and Hope

As I have researched and lectured and written about spiritual resiliency for many years, I've learned that spiritual health is far more complicated and difficult to describe than physical health. Part of the difficulty arises because we sometimes feel constrained to speak of our faith in exclusively positive terms, feeling that we will not be "good Christians" if we admit to doubts, discouragement, and fear. In the eyes of others, and even in our own eyes, we want to be Mother Teresa, while inside we recognize we are more like

When I wonder what has become of the personal suffering and brokenness of those I care for, I have a place to focus—namely, on the broken body of Christ. Paradoxically, it is on the cross of shame that dignity and grace are perfectly visible.

David, needing a fresh start and begging God to blot out our transgressions (Psalm 51).

Other complications arise because of the diverse way that spiritual ideas meet our everyday language and thought. For example, in Western culture we are highly prone to speaking of our relationship with God in individualistic terms, even though spiritual resiliency is seldom found in the individual alone. A central theme in this book is the importance of community, both as the place where resources and experiences for persons with dementia and their families can best be found, but also as spiritual community, as the body of Christ.

Perhaps you have a problem with the very word used to name this series of books, *hope*. Caregivers of folks with dementia must learn to live in the moment. If we are too future oriented, hope can be lost. Yet, we cling to God's promises and anticipate a better future, a hope beyond our days of toil and suffering. No cheap and easy sense of hope is satisfactory for those living with dementia, for we must somehow reconcile the event of God breaking into our world to bring us moments of joy, here and now, with the incomplete nature of creation and our longing for the fulfillment of God's reign. We might feel a tension between the present and the future. Christians wish to hear echoes of "consider the lilies of the field" (Matt 6:28) and thus be in the present without high anxiety, but we also believe "you do not grieve as those who have no hope" (1 Thess 4:13), and thus we lean into a future based on God's promises. Accepting the paradox of "already/not yet" is so important to the mature Christian life.

These tensions are at the heart of the Christian experience, including the work of caregiving and the challenge of living with a frightening diagnosis. But if we are committed to speaking the truth, if we can envision our lives as part of a community larger than ourselves, if we can live with the complexity of our position between yesterday, today, and tomorrow, and if we allow the Holy Spirit to guide our imaginations, we will be on our way to the spiritual resiliency we sorely need to meet the enormous challenge of living with dementia.

1

What I Want Most Is Respect: Dignity and Life with Dementia

I FIRST met Mr. K when his wife brought him to my counseling office. I was a new marriage-and-family therapist who had just begun my graduate work in gerontology. Mrs. K began by telling me, "He has Alzheimer's disease, and I think he needs someone to talk to."

Mr. K was my first private-practice client with dementia, and I remember feeling a bit uneasy as we began. Tall, handsome, and obviously feeling out of his element, he was one of the most physically impressive men over seventy I had met. I quickly learned that my new client did want someone to listen but also that he often could not organize his conversation to tell me a story that hung together. Whatever would I do with the fifty minutes we were scheduled to be together each week?

Mrs. K told me that her husband had served in the army during WWI, so the second week I decided to bring in old *Life* magazines, mostly from that period. This seemed to make the session far easier for both of us. Mr. K became quite animated and talkative as we paged through the magazines together. He recognized either the headlines or the context, such as photos of GIs and their jeeps in Europe. I began to look forward to our time together, even though he was not able to recall my name from week to week or remember what we had talked about. After a few weeks, he began smiling when he arrived, and I took that as a sign that our relationship was going well.

Gradually, Mr. K started confiding his feelings to me, saying, "My wife doesn't let me do what I want; she's babying me!" He seemed to view her as controlling and patronizing; he felt disrespected and out of control. He particularly hated not being able to drive, a loss I have learned is tough on many older persons. But what I remember most clearly about Mr. K was his ability to tell me what he needed: "Love is good, but what I want most is respect!" He said this several times during each session, so I had to attend to his words and take them seriously.

Some family sessions followed, conversations he quickly forgot but that seemed to be helpful to Mrs. K. She knew he was often angry, but she said she didn't realize he felt disrespected. She asked for a private session and then told me he had been a difficult man all their married life, short-tempered and sometimes verbally abusive. She admitted that it was a relief to her to be in charge now. He wanted respect, but she didn't feel she had received it herself throughout their marriage. Encouraging dignity in this relationship was far more complicated than I first realized when I was focused primarily on one side of the story!

In this part of the book, I will be exploring the tremendously important topic of dignity, particularly as it relates to people living with dementia and their caregivers. As the story above reveals, dignity is a basic human need, one that does not leave us at any stage or condition of life.

As I learned from Mr. and Mrs. K, dignity within our closest relationships can be complex and difficult to come by. All our dignity stories have a history. Some people desire respect more than love, and granting someone personal dignity doesn't always follow automatically from feeling affection for them. Husband and wife, adult child and parent, two close friends—any intimate relationship is impossible to fully understand from the outside. These partnerships have nuanced dynamics that even the participants seldom understand fully. Complicating these relationships even more are the challenges that arise when dementia is present, such

> Dignity is a basic human need, one that does not leave us at any stage or condition of life.

as confusion, increased dependency, and changed roles. How do persons live together with dignity, as caregivers and as persons needing care—particularly after a lifetime of imperfect relating?

What Is Dignity?

Jackie Robinson once said, "The most luxurious possession, the richest treasure anybody has, is his personal dignity."[1] What was Mr. K asking for when he asked for respect, if not that people relate to him as a person with dignity? What was Mrs. K pointing to when she said she was never respected in the marriage? Dignity is a gift we live into; respect is the way we acknowledge that dignity in others. Typically, dignity finds its way into our conversations when it is *not* present—when we are lamenting the disrespectful way we or someone else is being treated. According to Wikipedia, the English word *dignity*, "in ordinary modern usage, denotes 'respect' and 'status,' and it is often used to suggest that someone is not receiving a proper degree of respect, or even that they are failing to treat themselves with proper self-respect."[2]

I prefer to speak of *living with dignity*, rather than *having dignity*. Dignity is a living, vibrant experience that is deeply relational. I believe that it is through our lifelong relationships with others that we discover the feelings of self-worth and self-respect that we need for a happy life. We live with dignity both when those around us recognize we are worthy of respect and when we exercise respect for ourselves (see chapter 2). Another way to express these ideas is that living with dignity is dwelling in *the space between* two members of a relationship—without attempting to colonize (take over) that space. Dignity happens when two persons grant each other space and time to be both connected and separate from each other. This space has sometimes been labeled "intersubjective space,"[3] because it occurs when both persons in the relationship are subjects and no one feels like an object. This space is not granted when, for example, behaviors such as sexual abuse, patriarchy, and tyranny are present.

Dignity is a gift we live into; respect is the way we acknowledge that dignity in others.

The marvelous result of such a relationship is that living with dignity remains possible even when roles are different, the passing of time changes aspects of us (as with dementia), and features of the world around us shift (as when society changes its norms). I believe this experience of intersubjective space was what both Mr. and Mrs. K were longing for in their intimate relationship.

In a perfect world, all relationships would take place in this relational space, within mutual safety and respect. But as a marriage-and-family counselor, I am quite aware that this far from true. Perhaps the only place we find it possible to experience genuine life with dignity is in the one relationship that is completely trustworthy—our relationship with God.

The Foundations of Life with Dignity

"There is no longer Jew or Greek, there is no longer slave or free, there is no longer male and female; for all of you are one in Christ Jesus" (Gal 3:28). The apostle Paul wrote elegantly about his conviction that we are one in Christ. He was troubled because, in his lifetime, some Christians wanted to make distinctions, particularly between Jews and gentiles—a distinction that no longer made any sense to him after his conversion. This verse has inspired many Christians to advocate and struggle for human rights, including around issues of racial and gender equality. But I think Paul would be just fine with my adding, "neither those who are struggling with memory impairment, and those who are not" to his list. We are all one in Christ, and that is the foundation for our dignity.

Each person of faith understands their relationship with God differently and describes it with unique language. We rely on our personal experiences and the language of our faith traditions to provide words for this intimacy, which is often difficult to articulate. As a Lutheran Christian, I speak of living with dignity as God's gift to me, as an integral part of who I am as God's child because I was created in God's image. Accepting my own dignity has been one

Dignity is a living, vibrant experience that is deeply relational.

of my most important steps toward mature discipleship. Dignity is a gift I was given even before I was born and a gift that will accompany me throughout life, including the day that I die.

Because of this gift, which I neither earned nor deserve, I don't need to wonder what personal traits or accomplishments make me worthy of respect. Rather, I can count on God's promises to counter my fears and shame and help me recognize my status—promises such as "No longer do I call you servants, for the servant does not know what his master is doing; but I have called you friends" (John 15:15).

My dignity begins with creation. I believe that "God has made me and all creatures."[4] I am part of the marvelous diversity of creation. I celebrate a diversity that is cognitive as well as ethnic, sexual, religious, and age-based. If in my latter years, I develop dementia and am no longer able to make choices for myself, moral or otherwise, I will remain precious in the sight of God, who created me for good.

Second, I believe that God redeemed me through the work of Jesus Christ. Not because I am morally superior, but while I was yet a sinner, Christ died and rose for me (Rom 5:8), defeating not only death but all the forces of corruption and ugliness that threaten to hide my created dignity. As a redeemed person, I am part of the grateful group of sinners and saints whose status was restored on the cross and confirmed by an empty tomb, once for all, through the work of Christ, the suffering servant. His dignity covers me and renews my own.

I also believe that I can live with dignity because I have been welcomed into the body of Christ, the church. As a baptized child of God, I have the status that comes through the work of the Holy Spirit. I am God's own child, sealed with the cross of Christ forever! I am bound to other Christians throughout time and space by means of God's power. Nothing can rob me of this invisible bond or of the identity Christ earned for me.

There is no longer Jew or Greek, there is no longer slave or free, there is no longer male and female; for all of you are one in Christ Jesus.

Thus dignity, for me, goes far beyond any personal capacity—moral, intellectual, or physical. When I celebrate my status in the world, I celebrate not myself but rather the work of the Holy Trinity. The word of God has taught me that I am not dependent on my own thoughts or works to live with joy and peace. Rather, I can rejoice in the equal, dynamic, and respectful relationships deep within the life of God.

These proclamations are more than words for Christians. They are the basis for our very lives and our belief in human dignity. As we search for a reason to respect those who can no longer remember their loved ones' names or make decisions for themselves, we need look no further than the overflowing love of God, who creates, redeems, and unites us all. But how might this foundation for dignity play out in our imperfect, unjust world?

How Does Our Society Challenge Dignity?

Because of human brokenness, there are always those in society who attempt to diminish the dignity of others. Racism, ageism, and sexism are only a few of the ways vulnerable persons are stigmatized and disrespected. Sometimes this brokenness becomes normative in a society. The history of the world is filled with episodes when those in positions of power have completely ignored human dignity to horrific ends. At other times, disrespect is less obvious, lying below the surface but nonetheless harmful in the lives of its victims. I believe that whenever a person is treated as less than a whole person, God's heart is broken; each time a person becomes the victim of disrespect, they become part of the wounds of Christ's body.

Many courageous individuals have tried to educate the world about their need for dignity, reaching out to others with stories of their own struggles. One such person is Richard Taylor, who wrote about his experience with Alzheimer's disease.[5] Before his death in 2015, he spent much time and energy speaking about his dementia journey. In the introduction to a friend's book, Taylor

As we search for a reason to respect those who can no longer remember their loved ones' names or make decisions for themselves, we need look no further than the overflowing love of God.

used the metaphor of the mighty oak sprouting from the tiny acorn to encourage us all to work together to change the minds of those who do not understand how disrespect hurts people struggling with dementia:

> Concluding that the stigmas associated with the symptoms and label of dementia (I am fading away, I will die a shell of myself, I am more to be pitied than censured . . .) are reversible, we each in our own ways have become evangelists for a set of beliefs that is based on the fact that everyone is always a whole person until about 2 or 3 minutes after he or she has drawn a last breath.[6]

One of the primary goals of this book is to participate in this evangelism. I firmly believe that an increased appreciation for human dignity can contribute to resiliency in the everyday lives of those living with dementia. I begin by suggesting why dementia makes people particularly vulnerable to disrespect.

How Does Living with Dementia Challenge Personal Dignity?

Along with human sinfulness, there are situational challenges to personal dignity for both caregivers and the persons they care for when dementia is present. Some are experienced by all persons who are chronically ill and the persons who care for them, even without dementia. As a former full-time caregiver myself, I know how isolating and challenging this role can be. A caregiver must find ways to pay attention to the task at hand and to the diverse and pressing demands from the rest of her life—professional responsibilities, the needs of other family members, neighborhood and community involvement, congregational participation, and so forth. Since others in our social and family groups do not witness firsthand the work we are doing to give care, they may ask polite or even compassionate questions at first—"How is Tom doing?"—but soon life goes on as always, and our pressing needs as caregivers tend to be overlooked. If we become overwhelmed, we end up feeling that we are inadequate at fulfilling all our responsibilities or we become physically ill. The rate of serious illness for caregivers is frighteningly high; 60 percent of persons caring for someone with Alzheimer's report that they have concerns about their own health.[7]

To stay resilient, caregivers need many tangible resources, but they also need the intangible benefits of support and affirmation. I remember how moved and encouraged I was by my stepson's affirmation of me—"You are a very loving person"—when I first began caring for his grandfather, my father-in-law. I never told other family members what Jason said, but I often thought of it and felt encouraged, especially on those days when I didn't feel very loving. It is not as though we caregivers are motivated primarily by these comments. We do what we do for a variety of reasons, often simply because someone needs to step forward, or because, as in my case, we love the person to whom we are giving care. But a few simple words of acknowledgment and appreciation go a long way toward building self-respect, satisfying our sense of dignity and self-esteem in this nearly invisible work. Yet, most of us never think to give direct affirmation to someone who gives care, day after day.

Caregiving is always a challenge, but when dementia is present, it can lead to striking feelings of isolation and self-blame. Since supportive relationships are crucial to the development of resiliency,[8] pulling back from positive interactions with others works against maintaining our ability to "bounce back" during times of stress. During my interviews for this book, I heard stories of how the person experiencing dementia resisted going out in public, even to attend church services, and thus both caregiver and care recipient stayed home more. Some no longer wanted visitors and wanted the caregiver to be the sole person at home. One couple providing care for a loved one described how they had to take turns going to church services and no longer had a social life with friends.

At times, it is the caregiver himself who pulls back, unsure of how to handle the dementia in public. "I'm afraid she'll say something rude, or even curse, around other people," a client told me to explain why he no longer went out with his wife of many years who

All caregivers can use more relaxation and less stress in their lives. See the resources section at the end of this book for some ideas!

had early stage dementia. Role loss is another aspect of this self-isolation. When a caregiver must withdraw from their professional contacts, they can experience an additional loss of self-respect and daily affirmation because of role loss. And for married people, no longer being viewed as a member of an actively engaged couple can be itself a blow to personal dignity when one of the partners has received a large portion of self-worth by being part of a unit.

On the other hand, the one who receives care is often at even greater risk for losses in personal dignity. Anyone who has ever been a patient in a hospital knows of the many indignities experienced in a health-care setting, often despite the good intentions of the medical staff and persons such as "patient representatives." Even at home, it is difficult to feel respected when other people must help us walk, feed us, or assist us with toileting. I suspect that concerns about maintaining dignity are at the root of the frequent comment, "I hate the idea of having to be dependent on my children someday!"

Dementia makes it doubly challenging to live with dignity when receiving care. It is not easy to be dependent in our society,[9] and it is easy to internalize a sense of shame when we must ask for help. Persons experiencing dementia experience high levels of vulnerability, all day, every day. A person with dementia has trouble recognizing structure or remembering places and events consistently. The world becomes a frightening place. How could it be otherwise? When we don't feel safe or confident, we feel frightened, out of control, and inadequate. How easy it is to understand outbursts of anger in some folks with dementia as reflections of their intense fear.

Fortunately, although there is no cure for most forms of dementia, there are numerous strategies for enhancing dignity in both caregivers and persons with dementia. In the next chapter, I will share some helpful ways of thinking and behaving, shared with me by courageous men and women who have told me their stories of life with dementia. But first we must take an honest look at the realities we are up against, as both caregivers and care recipients.

Dementia makes it doubly challenging to live with dignity when receiving care. It is not easy to be dependent in our society,[9] and it is easy to internalize a sense of shame when we must ask for help.

"I Am No Longer a Wife": Dignity for the Caregiver

Many years ago, I read a story about a woman whose husband had been diagnosed with Alzheimer's disease. He became sexually abusive to her while she was caring for him, raping her and disrespecting her in numerous ways.[10] What seemed most painful to her was the fact that this was no longer the gentle, kind man she had married and was intimate with for so many years. She was committed to his care and had no plans to desert him, but she decided she could only continue to respect herself and continue her work if she imaged her role as a caregiver, no longer as a wife. She decided to create a private ritual in which she removed her wedding ring from her finger. Her ritual was not an isolated example. As marriage extends for many years, people find new ways to develop rituals.

As sad as this story is (and as different as it is from what some of us can imagine doing), it emphasizes the human capacity to discover dignity in urgent situations. It also speaks of the power of symbols and the ability to use creativity and maturity to survive a potentially tragic experience. Love for this resilient woman was no longer a romantic experience, no longer part of her vision of marriage when she was a young bride or a new mother. Instead it took the form of loyalty, acceptance, and self-respect as a caregiver.

The need for personal dignity lies below the surface in many caregiving stories. Sadly, this need for caregivers is seldom addressed, and little guidance is given to caregivers who are living through private traumas of great urgency. There is a growing body of literature focused on the need to enhance dignity for persons experiencing dementia,[11] but the dignity of caregivers has received far too little attention. Both are crucially important, for if a caregiver does not practice self-respect, or receive validation for her work, it is nearly impossible to experience hope rather than despair, satisfaction rather than discontent, and peace rather than constant regrets. Caregiver abuse is also, of course, far more likely to occur in relationships lacking in mutual respect.

Abuse by caregivers can also arise from their own poor self-care, and this is often discussed in caregiving literature. The link between paying adequate attention to one's own basic needs for good health and the importance of living with dignity is often mentioned. If we feel good about ourselves, we care for ourselves—creating a positive cycle of health. But if we do not practice adequate self-care, a reverse cycle (poor self-care followed by less self-respect) also occurs. As a pastor and counselor and as an interviewer for this book, I was distressed to hear frequent confessions of inadequate self-care. Some of the reasons for ignoring one's own needs are practical, such as limited financial resources and an inadequate support network. Yet, too often caregivers are not proactive or persistent in searching for resources beyond the most obvious. Frequently, resources in congregations, communities, and family networks are not explored. As I reread my notes from the interviews I conducted for this book, I began wondering about the tendency to simply accept the situation and not look for needed help. Could it be that dignity has something to do with this problem?

It is important to note that the actual tasks of caregiving can contribute to feelings that one is losing dignity. One woman I interviewed began by saying, "What mess do you want to hear about first?" She looked both tired and discouraged, and I discovered she wasn't caring for herself physically or emotionally. Her idea that caregiving revolved around "messes" spoke of her attempt to be honest but also of her tendency to reduce all that she did to the unpleasant, physical aspects of her daily experiences. Or perhaps she was simply having a bad day!

I believe that there are ways to be realistic about caregiving but also recognize that the value of our work is determined, in part, by the narratives of care we tell ourselves. Are they sufficiently complex to avoid seeing ourselves stuck in a particular role, such as victim? In the following chapter, I suggest that some ways we talk to ourselves are not helping. Simplistic plot lines and rigid roles of martyr or victim can rob us of basic motivation for self-care. I believe it is possible to become more resilient simply by telling ourselves stories

If we feel good about ourselves, we care for ourselves—creating a positive cycle of health. But if we do not practice adequate self-care, a reverse cycle (poor self-care followed by less self-respect) also occurs.

about healthier, more flexible behavior in which our problems are externalized, our primary status is being a child of God, and the plot lines of our narrative are more complex and hopeful than we first believed.

Dignity for the Person Experiencing Dementia

It is difficult to imagine a circumstance that challenges personal dignity more than dementia. Many of us find as we age that we are forgetting our own phone number or the name of a close friend, and we make jokes about growing old and forgetful. But for someone with serious difficulties remembering, each lapse can become a source of potential embarrassment since it is likely to be interpreted as a symptom of dementia. Vulnerability increases dramatically in late stages of dementia when a person must depend totally on others for simple acts such as covering his body or assisting with toilet needs. We all wish to be spoken to with a respectful tone of voice, but that, too, is sometimes beyond the control of many persons with dementia, as in the case of very fragile persons in some long term care facilities (often staffed by untrained, under paid, and exhausted nurse's aides). During these vulnerable days of life, the person experiencing dementia cannot directly express the need to be treated with respect, and family members and friends must become dignity advocates.

An Invitation and Gift

Each chapter of this book concludes with a meditation on a psalm. I made the decision to emphasize the psalms in this way for two primary reasons. First, I am aware that, in my own life, it has been the psalms that sustained me at times of personal crisis. At those times, I would sit and simply read the psalms over and over again, as God began to heal me. My second reason is what I learned from listening to caregivers as a counselor, and to professional caregivers as a seminary professor—namely, that psalms hold unique power for many people. I am hoping that perhaps you, as you give care, might choose to share portions of these meditations with the person you are caring for, if and when that is possible and appropriate.

But I write here primarily for you, the one who has taken up this enormous task of giving care. Your amazing love in action is always before me as I reflect on how God's love empowers us all.

Reflection on Psalm 23

The Lord is my shepherd;
I shall not want.
He makes me to lie down in green pastures;
He leads me beside the still waters.
He restores my soul;
He leads me in the paths of righteousness
For his name's sake.
Yea, though I walk through the valley of the shadow of death,
I will fear no evil;
For you are with me;
Your rod and your staff they comfort me.
You prepare a table before me in the presence of my enemies;
You anoint my head with oil;
My cup runs over.
Surely goodness and mercy will follow me
All the days of my life;
And I will dwell in the house of the Lord
Forever. (NKJV)

WE HAVE heard this psalm so often that it is hard to actually hear the words. At funerals, around death beds, at times of national crisis, Psalm 23 has become almost a secular text—it is well-known, even by people who are unacquainted with other parts of the Bible. But now I invite you to meditate with me on this psalm from a caregiver's perspective, for Psalm 23 speaks to us not only at times of death but also in our everyday lives, as we face everyday fears and needs.

This is a psalm about trust. The power these words have had through generations, and across many nations of the world, comes from the beautiful, loving image of a Shepherd who keeps us safe with his rod and staff, who leads us calmly past troubled waters, who prepares for us a banquet of all that we need and who never leaves our side. This Shepherd is a leader who knows that each day we are crossing narrow chasms, dangerous and filled with predators. He knows that we often wander off and need to be pulled back into safety. And he knows we are at the greatest risk when we are spiritually alone, without the presence of the One who loves, saves, and feeds us.

The Shepherd of Psalm 23 is not an idea, not an abstract concept, but the One with whom we can have a living relationship. The psalm is about trust not in a dogma or creed but in a living, caring God. This Shepherd has a face, the face that never goes away. Even the faces of those we love, our parents, our friends, partners, colleagues, beloved family members, will all eventually go away. No person can always be there to pull us back from dangers or keep us on the safe path. But the face of the Shepherd will never leave us. And so we can trust this Shepherd. We can trust that even when we wander off and behave no better than stupid sheep, the One who loves us will still be there—forgiving, guiding, giving us all that we need.

Psalm 23 is not a sentimental psalm, no matter how it is presented in a secular world. Its words should not make us feel cozy and warm, as though the Shepherd were our personal servant. Christianity is not a feel-good religion. As we hear these words, we are not left with a stupid smile on our faces. The words are comforting but also tough. After all, we hear about crossing the valley of the shadow of death (both a valley of actual death but also a valley filled with all those dark things that try to keep us from light and truth). The psalmist speaks of actual enemies who do not wish us well. What he faces is terrifying evil—the dark side that can easily harm us, especially when we bow to its power. There is nothing sentimental about Psalm 23.

We can trust that even when we wander off and behave no better than stupid sheep, the One who loves us will still be there—forgiving, guiding, giving us all that we need.

Each generation has heard this psalm in a different context. Martin Luther preached about it over dinner (poor Katie—I'm sure the food was cold before he finished!). He envisioned the banquet that the Good Shepherd prepared for us as the word of God, the word of nurture that we can feast upon because it is the good news that we are forgiven. Luther believed passionately that we have as our God not a harsh condemning judge but a tender, loving Shepherd.

This loving Shepherd is there precisely because there has always been evil in the world. But perhaps what is most distressing is that we seem so ill prepared to deal with evil. In so many ways we are confused, dealing with fears, insecurities, and fragmented relationships. Where is trust in the Good Shepherd? Whose rod and staff are guiding us?

I am comforted by remembering that although the dark forces will always be with us, there are some persons who have modeled for us what it is to walk in the light, what it is to trust in the Good Shepherd. We think of Desmond Tutu, who resisted the dark powers of apartheid and courageously worked for truth and reconciliation in his country. Or our own Abraham Lincoln, who rose out of humble circumstances to take on the forces that would keep the dreadful system of slavery going in our land. Or Mother Teresa, whose whole life reflected her following of the Good Shepherd, as she ministered to the most vulnerable persons in Calcutta. But many times those who faithfully follow the Good Shepherd do not make headlines and are never know by others outside their own communities.

Who has been the model for you? Who has taught you what it looks like to trust in the One who loves, saves, and redeems us? I was fortunate enough to meet such a model while I was doing research for a book on spiritual resiliency. His name was Wilhelm, and he was a physician living out his retirement quietly in his little city of Göttingen, Germany. Raised in a pastor's family, Wilhelm had memories of the risks his father took to follow God faithfully, first speaking out against Hitler, and then risking imprisonment simply

Who has taught you what it looks like to trust in the One who loves, saves, and redeems us?

for holding church services in his home after the Communists took over East Germany. Wilhelm told me that his walk with God has been a privilege, especially when he could speak of God's forgiveness to those who are troubled by their images of a harsh, unforgiving God. He told me of a conversation he had with a woman, dying of cancer, who was racked by guilt for an early sin. Said Wilhelm, "As I left the room, I was astonished by what I had said, and thankful to be allowed to be an instrument [of faith and comfort] to her because it is often hard to talk with people [about faith]."[1]

I believe that when we follow the Shepherd, when we trust in his guidance and love, we not only have personal peace but are equipped to pass it on. Perhaps the very fact that Psalm 23 is so well known creates a mission opportunity for us. Because of our loyalty to the Shepherd, we don't stop being ambassadors for Christ when we become caregivers. There are always people in our daily lives who need to hear a word of hope. Perhaps we have the chance to not only repeat these words but to talk about them and to live them, showing the world how trust in the Good Shepherd is revealed in everyday life. It is good to repeat them, because often by saying prayers or hymns over and over again they become truer for us. We learn to trust by saying and singing, "The Lord is my Shepherd."

On the other hand, when we make this psalm, or any other part of our faith, into a sentimental, self-serving recitation that ignores the evil surrounding us and the brokenness within us, we cheapen our beliefs and miss our opportunity to say to the world, *There is a Good Shepherd who will keep you safe; the good news is how much God loves and forgives you.* We must tell the world about this truth, because we have a promise for the world that alone can satisfy the anxious, lonely heart, the promise given at the end of this psalm. This is a promise for all the days of our lives, for all circumstances we experience, in sickness and in health, in war and in peace—the best promise ever made—that we will dwell in the house of the Lord forever.

There is a Good Shepherd who will keep you safe; the good news is how much God loves and forgives you.

If we trust this wild, crazy promise that is too good not to be true, we will be safe from evil. For trust, in my view, is the best antidote for evil. Fear and evil are bedfellows. It is at times of anxiety and fear that we are at our very worst, wandering off the path, hurting others, and trying to defend ourselves in injurious, childish ways. Think of your own life, and the times you have been at greatest risk of straying off the path of faith. What were you afraid of? Being shamed? Being found out? Not having enough power to change the things that cannot be changed?

When I was a child, I thought as a child (1 Cor 13:11). Psalm 23 was not composed for those with a childish faith. It is a powerful psalm for all the days of our lives, and for those of us who are older, it is a psalm of challenge as well as of comfort. How much can we trust God? This is the basic question we must ask ourselves every time we say these words. If the trust is not sufficient for life's unexpected challenges, then perhaps we need to say and sing this psalm more often, allowing these beautiful words to wash over us, heal us, and take away our fearful ways.

2

I Learned to Join in the Journey: Dignity as Accompaniment

HOW DO you picture your life? We all carry around mental pictures of our personal experiences, some more helpful than others. You may not have thought of your life in this way, but my years as a counselor have convinced me that we all create, without being fully aware of them, dominant roles and story lines for ourselves.

All stories have a tone (sad, funny, hopeful, and so forth), main characters (the hero, the villain, the victim, the rescuer, and so on) and either simplistic or complex ways of understanding events and human beings. So, too, our individual stories are uniquely designed around the plots and roles we have (unconsciously) chosen. We organize the events of our lives around the plots and roles of these hidden narratives. Most often, we create stories around our central role—for example, the hero or the victim. One problem with many of our narratives is their lack of complexity and flexibility, leading to black and white interpretations, without shades of grey and thus with little room for growth and wisdom.

Many of us who are either family or professional caregivers tend to think of ourselves in the role of savior or rescuer. Others of us feel more like victims and design our narratives around that role, as though it is the only one that fits us. There are clear challenges to both of these possibilities. Heroes get easily discouraged and worn out, and victims become passive and depressed. If we have cast ourselves in the role of victim, it is difficult to be proactive in giving care. If we see ourselves as a savior, it is difficult to face failures, even when they are beyond our control.

Elenore, who graciously shared her experiences with me in an interview for this book, began her caregiving by creating a story plot that was exhausting. She viewed herself as the "perfect daughter" who was totally responsible for her mother's welfare. Her mother was the victim in this story, the one acted upon, and Elenore was the heroine, the actor. For example, if her mother made a comment that was factually incorrect, it was Elenore's job, as savior, to correct her, to argue with the content. What a burden she was carrying!

But then Elenore attended a workshop for caregivers that changed her inner story dramatically. Before the workshop, she had already cared for her mother, who was living with vascular dementia, for five years. She loved her mother deeply, and they had always been close, but before the workshop, her role as heroine led Elenore to beleive that caring for her mother meant finding all necessary practical situations. Her inner plotline was one of resisting dementia and saving her mother. After the workshop, however, Elenore made a dramatic move from visualizing caregiving as a burden to thinking of caregiving as accompaniment. She did this simply by reflecting on a question that impacted her private narrative: What role must I assume as a caregiver of someone with dementia? To answer this question, she now rejected *rescuer* for *companion on the journey*.

In her new, more complex narrative, Elenore's mother was no longer the helpless object of her care. Her mother continued to need help, but she also became, for Elenore, a companion, a person to accompany on a strange journey. Now they were both actors, moving into the challenging adventure of living with dementia. Mutuality replaced obligation because they were now journeying together into an unknown future. Although many of Elenore's everyday responsibilities were unchanged, she was now more flexible in the ways she thought and talked about their relationship. This changed perspective meant, for example, that she could note and celebrate the ongoing nuances in her mother's personality, increasing her mother's dignity. The change to accompaniment also meant that Elenore could begin moving toward accepting her mother's diagnosis. So long as Elenore felt she had to save and fix her mother, she was stuck in denial and fear. Now she was in the role of friend and helper, who could participate in both joys and sorrows during the dementia journey. What a relief for this daughter, to leave those rigid, overly dramatic ways of being a caregiver behind.

The journey image started out as an abstraction, but became quite concrete for Elenore and her mother over time. They began to enjoy more playful and flexible experiences together. Inspired by the image offered at the facility where the training occurred (where an imitation train station was available for the residents to "ride"), Elenore traded in a story line of "I'll take care of you" for "Let's get on the train together!" Since her mother had always loved trains, this metaphor fit beautifully. Elenore had a new way of traveling with her mother into the coming days.

> You may need to "fire" yourself from a rigid role.

Is there an image that you could draw on to become more flexible and hopeful about the way you are imaging yourself as a caregiver? If you feel stuck in a role that lacks playfulness and flexibility, let alone mutual respect, you might want to do a little editing of your own caregiving story. You may need to "fire" yourself from a rigid role. Perhaps some special interest of the person you are accompanying will aid your imagination here, as the train journey did for Elenore.

Reimaging Dignity as Mutuality

Elenore's revelation became, through our conversation, one of my own. One of the gifts I received from her and from other caregivers who shared their stories with me was an increased appreciation for a strong connection between dignity and mutuality. Rather than picturing dignity as an abstract, independent quality in each person, I began to understand that dignity is not something we have but something we live. It is a dynamic experience that colors all our lives as we share it with those around us. As I thought about what I was hearing from caregivers like Elenore, I began to make connections between the amazing respect they had for the persons who need their care and their ability to accompany, to join with them on life's journey as mutually vulnerable human beings.

Elenore's mother, Claire, died two years before I interviewed Elenore. She had made her final goodbye to her mother after nine years of caregiving. The last days were sad, she told me, but she had far fewer regrets after learning to treasure the times they had together, especially after her conversion to accompaniment.

Elenore now tells the story of her journey along with her mother as a complex experience. She described her mother as a classy, feisty woman who was highly respected and involved in her church and community. Having experienced her mother's powerful personality throughout her life, neither Elenore nor her siblings could easily accept the signs of dementia as they first appeared. But when Claire became more confused and dependent, her children decided to move her to assisted living, then a nursing home, and finally, in the last months, to total care. "We never moved her until it was absolutely necessary that she have more care," Elenore explained. Clearly, the respect she and her siblings had for their mother informed their decision to choose venues that would permit as much quality of life and independence as possible. Perhaps there is a link between the appropriate level of care and the maximum level of independence provided, as one continuing-care community director has suggested.[1]

Caregiving for someone with dementia is never an easy journey, and Elenore's was no exception. Over the years, Elenore told me, she experienced a variety of emotional reactions as she moved from tears and resistance to increased peace and acceptance. During the early years, she constantly corrected her mother's mistakes, and tried to deny the dementia, saying things such as, "Mother, you know today is Tuesday, not Saturday!" Fear, shame, a need to fix and save

> Dignity is not something we have but something we live.

were reasons she gave for her early style of caregiving. Denial was an understandable obstacle. A particularly painful memory was that of a morning when Elenore called her mother (who was still living alone at that point) and invited her to lunch. When she got to her mother's house, not only had her mother completely forgotten she had lunch plans with Elenore, but she had already gone out for a meal with Elenore's brother. Elenore admitted, "I went home and cried." She didn't explain her tears to me, but I suspect they were tears of grief as she began to realize the dementia was real. Perhaps there was also a bit of sibling rivalry tucked in, since we never are quite free of those primal feelings—in fact, they can be more common under the stress of caregiving.

After the workshop, however, Elenore changed her whole approach to caregiving. Instead of merely stopping at her mother's apartment to check on her physical condition, Elenore would pack lunches and take her mother out for picnics or to coffee shops. She told me that as soon as she stopped arguing, she and her mom were suddenly able to have fun together. She had fired herself from the role of fixer, stopped arguing about incorrect context in her mother's comments, and learned to enter her mother's world. Learning a few basic communication skills from the workshop was also helpful—for example, going with the emotions expressed or redirecting a memory for the impaired person who is becoming agitated (see below).

Elenore smiled often during the interview as she told me stories of the adventures they had during those years—adventures she believes would have never occurred without a new way of thinking of her role as caregiver. "One time I took mother up on the [Blue Ridge] Parkway, and we sat and looked at the fall leaves, not saying much at all." Elenore knew that she and her mother were on a journey without any itinerary and with an unknown destination, yet she was committed to going along for the ride, whatever came, enjoying each day insofar as possible. "The last days were difficult, but I am so grateful for the better times that we had along the way."

Elenore's respect for her mother was never an issue; she both loved and admired Claire. But until Elenore changed her inner narrative and freed herself from the unrealistic goals of fixing and saving, she could not relate to her mother in ways that were creative, genuine, and calm. Through her story, she convinced me that *accompaniment* is a far better way to live out our respect than trying to fix or save. Without the savior role, we can experience mutuality—the best way to be supportive to anyone, including our loved ones with dementia.

Mutuality and Dignity

It is not only caregivers who must rewrite their stories in the face of dementia. Perhaps you are yourself in the early stages of an illness that leads to cognitive impairments. You are slowly realizing that you must leave behind your life's work, relying on others to help you manage your finances and to remember your calendar. You worry that your days to come will have no real purpose as you begin to need other people more and more and contribute less and less to the their practical needs (or so it seems to you). Many of the roles that have made you feel good about yourself are slipping away, be it professional or volunteer or homemaker. In this situation, depression and meaninglessness are real possibilities.

Persons with dementia are forced to change their narratives even more dramatically than caregivers. "I am a successful physician" can become "I am the man someone else must dress and bathe." Dementia disrupts our dreams for the future, but also the timeline of our continuing stories—past, present, and future. Since it is hard to recall the past in the same chronological order as one's caregivers, since the demands of the present are often confusing, and since the future is totally unclear, it can be difficult to have a sense of empowerment. This disempowerment, in turn, threatens personal dignity. As two research nurses explain: "The illness story is wrecked because its present is not what the past was supposed to lead up to, and the future is scarcely thinkable."[2]

Dementia disrupts our dreams for the future, but also the timeline of our continuing stories— past, present, and future.

If you are facing these challenges, the last thing you want is to feel like an object of care rather than an agent, with choices and unique experiences. Perhaps you have found that even very kind people offend and hurt you from time to time. You may need to tell them that you don't need a savior, and you certainly don't want pity. You simply want someone to jump on the train with you, to make the journey as your companion.

Pity is so offensive; it is a cheap and easy way to keep a distance between ourselves and someone with special needs. Compassion, on the other hand, is first cousin of mutuality, since this word captures the "with you" aspect of a loving, respectful relationship. But even compassion needs to be expressed carefully, in ways that do not create distance or become disrespectful.

We can learn about the experience of dementia from moving outside this illness for a moment. I have the privilege to be friends with a colleague who lost his legs to cancer early in life. As I accompany him in a variety of circumstances, I notice the difference between those who, albeit with good intentions, treat him as an object of concern, and those who join with him in whatever comes along on the journey. The latter help when necessary and step back when he can manage for himself. My friend has strong self-esteem, and his life is rich, fruitful, and inspirational—in part because of his strong personality and Christian faith, and in part through the mutuality he finds in his relationships. He has taught me that, if we wish to live with purpose and meaning, we seek out relationships that enhance our dignity—those based on mutuality. We also are free to avoid those situations and people who would diminish us.

My friend has a remarkable ability to imagine his life in helpful, mature ways. Perhaps caregivers have more difficulty "getting" mutuality than those with special needs. But we can grow and change as we join others in their journeys, as Elenore did. I like to think about the ways her story was recreated, for the best, during her caregiving experiences. This work required so much courage and love! She grew personally as well as in her relationship with her

> If we wish to live with purpose and meaning, we seek out relationships that enhance our dignity— those based on mutuality.

mother. Ironically, one of the redemptive possibilities in caregiving is the ways it can mature those of us who have the privilege to provide care. Like Elenore's story, all our narratives can use a good rewrite now and then!

"Thou Shalt Not Argue!"

As Elenore's interview shows, editing our inner stories is only the first step. As we change our roles, we find ourselves communicating in different ways. But, to some caregivers, my suggestion that it is best not to argue with a person with dementia may sound unrealistic. Perhaps your father, who has Alzheimer's disease, is talking about going to work as though he were not retired. You worry that he will do something inappropriate unless you correct his memory, like try to walk or drive to his old work place (wandering is a common problem with memory impairment). How can you respond without getting into an argument or causing unnecessary grief? How can we understand why our desire to argue and correct is so strong in the first place?

Hard as it is to admit, the first thing we are up against in situations where we feel inclined to correct a person who is confused is our own desire to be right. We have been trained all our life to get our point across. But suddenly, as caregivers, being right is not the most important thing. Understanding the emotional message, rather than perfecting the factual content, becomes our goal. We can learn to refocus and redirect rather than correct and argue. What a new way to think and act!

Elenore shared examples of this important shift with me. Early on in her caregiving, she would become dismayed because her mother said something such as, "I need to call your father and tell him where I am!" Elenore would respond with a factual correction, "Mother, you know Daddy's been dead for seven years!" But after learning how to refocus and redirect, she changed her response from arguing to validating the feelings behind her mother's comment, "I know you really miss Daddy." What followed was no longer a

> The first thing we are up against in situations where we feel inclined to correct a person who is confused is our own desire to be right.

painful argument but an experience of shared feelings and mutual respect.

As a nursing-home chaplain, I used this strategy often. When a resident and an aide were arguing about going to an activity, for example, I would try to steer the conversation slightly off target from the immediate power struggle. Perhaps a comment about how much Mrs. Jones enjoys waiting for visits from her grandchildren (which may be why she wants to stay in her room). Or, if someone says, "I have to go home and cook dinner," a response might be to ask what she likes to cook, rather than to correct her by saying, "You don't cook anymore—you live here now."

If you are thinking, "This is just too hard to do," it may be helpful to realize that many caregivers have faced this problem before you. Responding to this need, the Alzheimer's Association has created rich educational materials to help caregivers of those with dementia (not only those of someone with Alzheimer's). Here, for example, is a quote from an online newsletter on the topic, "Thou shalt not argue!"

> Do not try to reason! Do not confront! Do not point out they are wrong! Do not argue! Being right may lead you to failure. This is because patients with advancing dementia experience a decline in their reasoning skills while they experience an increase in emotional responses. Facts, dates, causes, consequences and logic become increasingly less important. Feelings, however, grow in importance and intensity.[3]

The good news about learning to validate rather than argue is that it is surprisingly easy to learn. And it is far more satisfying.

Communication for Those without Language

But what about situations when the person receiving our care can no longer speak, as in late stages of dementia? How can we not argue and instead join the journey—communicate our compassion and maintain dignity—when we can't listen because our loved one can no longer speak? As with every stage of dementia care, but especially during the advanced stages, practical knowledge, a calm demeanor, and a beginner's mind are necessary for caregiving that is open, flexible, and respectful. Here, too, I have learned from caregivers who were gracious enough to share their experiences with me. They told me of times when they were able to sit calmly with their mute loved one, quietly holding hands or stroking a cheek.

Have you ever considered how important nonverbal communication is when we relate to each other, with or without dementia? Even when we don't have thinking problems, we express ourselves primarily without words. Think of how much you learn from your close friend (to say nothing of your pets) by simply searching a face, picking up on a tone of voice, or noting how often she contacts you. Communication expert Albert Mehrabian suggests that only 7 percent of our communication is conveyed with words. Vocal elements such as tone and volume convey 38 percent, and 55 percent comes through nonverbal facial expressions, gesture, posture,

Tools for Communication

1. Help them explore their spiritual gifts and how they use them.

2. To enhance dignity, apologize when you don't recognize what is being said.

3. Don't hesitate to repeat questions, perhaps using different words.

4. Do not become impatient and interrupt or speak over the other person.

5. Use simple terms, short sentences, or gestures, such as "Did you brush your hair?"

6. Be playful and use humor. Laugh at life together!

7. When words fail, invite the person to act out what she wants or needs.

and the like. That means that 93 percent of our interactions with another person are nonverbal![4]

Often, the silent ways we communicate are more important than the content of our conversations. As anyone who has been hospitalized for a serious illness knows, having someone simply sit quietly by your bedside is a powerful way to say, "I love you; I'm with you." Sadly, I have heard professional caregivers (including clergy) state that they no longer visit a person with late-stage dementia because "She doesn't say anything. She doesn't even know I'm here." This is wrong on so many levels, including the fact that most persons with late-stage dementia *do* have ways to understand and even, at times, to respond nonverbally—long after spoken language is impossible. Sometimes there are even moments of speaking after long periods of silence: many pastors, including myself, have stories of a person who has not said a word in years suddenly joining in with Psalm 23 or the Lord's Prayer.

When Dementia Has Advanced

What does this journey of accompaniment look like when caregivers are caring for a severely impaired loved one 24/7? A visit with Sam and Sally provided me with a glimpse of that experience. This couple, both retired professionals, graciously invited me to meet with them in the home they now share with Katherine, Sam's ninety-four-year-old mother. She was diagnosed with Alzheimer's disease more than nine years ago and has been living with them for the past two years. During my visit, we sat in the living room while Katherine napped in a reclining chair in the adjacent family room.

My initial impression was that this couple was devoted to Katherine but that they were also physically and emotionally exhausted. They clearly needed and wanted to talk and to share with someone the details of the devoted care they provided, but they looked and sounded very tired. They proudly showed me the electric lift they had recently installed going from the main floor to the basement

> Most persons with late-stage dementia *do* have ways to understand and even, at times, to respond nonverbally—long after spoken language is impossible.

bedroom where Katherine sleeps, and told stories of faithful attention to all her needs.

But their narratives were also filled with images of burden, fatigue, and helplessness. They visualized themselves as locked into a daily round of responsibilities because of Katherine's high dependency on them. Bathing, feeding, giving medicines as scheduled, and transporting Katherine upstairs and downstairs on the mechanical lift are just a few of the nonstop caregiving activities in their lives.

Fortunately, they have each other and work as a team, with Sally, who is an RN, playing the role of organizer and director. But they need relief, and extended family is largely absent. Sam's sister no longer comes to help because "she says she can't manage emotionally, seeing our mother now." Their adult son is "busy with his own life." When I asked Sally what she was hoping for, she said, "To be able to go out to dinner with my husband now and then." I began to feel tired and helpless just hearing this couple's story.

I confess that, at several points in the conversation, I couldn't resist stepping out of my researcher/writer role to encourage them to find respite. I told them about the Alzheimer's Association and support groups, both in person and online, and they seemed curious and interested. I was surprised that they had not already taken advantage of even the most basic resources available, but I am learning that many families see dementia as a private matter and hesitate to reach outside the family for help.

Faith is obviously a pillar for this couple, and at the core of their resiliency. They are confident that God will give them the strength needed for a difficult task. They spoke of their faith in the same matter-of-fact tone that they used to describe Katherine and their caregiving work—they didn't smile or laugh or cry often. I sensed it was taking all their energy just to do the work they needed to do each day.

But then the interview shifted: Sally left the room briefly, and I asked Sam what he hoped for, just as I asked Sally and all my respondents. My instincts told me that he would be more open without his wife in the room. To my surprise, he began to weep, "I just hope we never have to place my mother in a nursing home. I've seen those places, and I don't ever want that for her." Here was a man who was grieving and worrying, even as he provided amazing around-the-clock care. Was he worrying that his wife, or that he himself, would run out of energy for their task, or that Katherine's condition would continue to decline and make it impossible to keep her at home? I never found out, because just then Sally returned to the room and he changed the subject abruptly.

Later, there was another important moment. As I was leaving, they asked if I would like to meet Katherine. They told me she "might not be able to say much," and we went into the family room where she was sitting and had been napping. She sat bent over in her chair and was obviously fragile. They spoke to her quietly, stroking her hand gently, and introduced me by my first name. What they showed me was a wonderful example of nonverbal communication, of love in action.

After a few words with Katherine, I suggested we all hold hands to pray together. As I asked God to strengthen them and Katherine, and to bless their work, Sam again cried silently. I felt any words were inadequate in the face of so much love and suffering, in the face of Sam's grief and Sally's fatigue. But it was clear to me that God was present in this home and in this moment, because God, above all others, understands our tears as much as our words.

I remain concerned about this very tired, devoted, and isolated couple. I hope they will call the Alzheimer's Association and begin taking advantage of its rich resources. And I hope that, as I encouraged them, they will let their pastor know more directly what they need from the congregation. Above all, I hope that Sam and Sally realize that the love and devotion they show, day after day, constitutes a life of discipleship, a "called life."[5] I pray that we, as a church, continue to find ways to support caregivers who so desperately need both our spiritual and practical support, including

Perhaps prayers that include "sighs too deep for words" (Rom 8:26) are the most important nonverbal communications of all.

holding up caregiving as a vocation that is just as important as any other.

If Martin Luther affirmed the vocation of a father who changed his child's diaper, then surely the church that bears his name can affirm the humble work of those who care for persons with advanced dementia. (Luther's words are also remarkable for their gender equality—he would have applauded the involvement of Sam as well as Sally.)

> Now you tell me, when a father goes ahead and washes diapers or performs some other mean task for his child, and someone ridicules him as an effeminate fool, though that father is acting in the spirit just described and in Christian faith, my dear fellow you tell me, which of the two is most keenly ridiculing the other? God, with all his angels and creatures, is smiling, not because that father is washing diapers, but because he is doing so in Christian faith.[6]

In the following chapter, I explore how the church might grow into a life together as we support both persons experiencing dementia and those who give care that makes the angels smile.

Reflection on Psalm 38:9–22

O Lord, all my longing is known to you;
my sighing is not hidden from you.
My heart throbs, my strength fails me;
as for the light of my eyes, it also has gone from me
My friends and companions stand aloof from my affliction,
and my neighbors stand far off.
Those who seek my life lay their snares;
those who seek to hurt me speak of ruin,
and meditate treachery all day long.
But I am like the deaf. I do not hear;
like the mute, who cannot speak.
Truly, I am like one who does not hear,
and in whose mouth, is no retort.
But it is for you, O Lord, that I wait;
it is you, O Lord my God, who will answer.
For I pray, "Only do not let them rejoice over me,
those who boast against me when my foot slips."
For I am ready to fall,
and my pain is ever with me.
I confess my iniquity;
I am sorry for my sin.
Those who are my foes without cause are mighty,
and many are those who hate me wrongfully.
Those who render me evil for good
are my adversaries because I follow the good.
Do not forsake me, O Lord;
O my God, do not be far from me;
Make haste to help me,
O Lord, my salvation. (X)

NOT EVERYONE has a companion for their journey with illness. Rather than exhibiting the playfulness of Elenore or the devotion of Sam and Sally, the caregivers who surrounded this psalmist have emotionally and physically deserted him. He is a pariah, outcast by others simply because he is sick. He is robbed of his dignity and his ability to be part of the human community. He laments that even his neighbors "stand far off."

It is difficult to read this psalm without feeling sad. Although we are separated from the psalmist by many years and by deep cultural and theological understandings, his throbbing heart and failing strength touch us deeply. Most of us have known the pain and the intense anxiety that accompany a serious illness. But mostly we grieve for his isolation. As if being sick were not enough, he is entirely alone, utterly cut off from those around him who are afraid to comfort him. What could possibly be worse? In the face of this anguish, we want to cry out, "Really! If things are that bad, how can you possibly trust in God!"

Does the psalmist have dementia? Not likely, since his illness is not identified and sounds more physical than mental. But the isolation and confusion he feels are much like the experiences of persons with impaired memories. "My pain is ever with me. . . . I am ready to fall. . . . My friends and companions stand aloof from my affliction." Constant pain (emotional and/or physical), the fear of literal falling, the knowledge that one is being ignored—no man or woman with dementia is a stranger to these experiences. The psalmist's cry is their own: "Make haste to help me, O Lord, my salvation."

Of course, it is not necessary to identify the specific illness of the psalmist, because what matters most, what inspires us powerfully across the centuries, is his incredible trust in deliverance. He looks for rescue from his difficult life. Reading this psalm, I immediately thought of the messy world of dementia care that emerged in the interviews for this book—stories I heard of courageous but imperfect solutions to everyday problems, bleak diagnoses, misunderstandings of friends and neighbors. Being human means facing illness as best we can, but the challenges make us want to cry out in lament.

Like those of us who give care, the writer of Psalm 38 does not expect a perfect world, even though his existence in this one is so difficult. He does not seem to demand physical healing, but only forgiveness for his sins. (In Old Testament times, sin and illness were closely tied together theologically.) He longs for spiritual healing. He needs forgiveness and an increased sense of God's presence, sometime soon. As my colleague Fred Gaiser wrote, "Psalm 38 seeks order and meaning as ways to combat illness. It provides movement, and it ends with hope."[1]

But how can there be order, let alone hope, when one is so upset that it is impossible even to speak to others? We are reminded again of the challenges of dementia—of the inability to respond with words, adding to social isolation. I have so often heard people speak of "hopelessness" when they see people with end-stage dementia sitting alone in a reclining chair, unable to speak. Similarly, the psalmist says that in his mouth there is "no retort." Order and hope, however, come from his ability to lament—to cry out to God, telling about the pain he feels. And, as he laments his pain, he begins to move past it.

> We know that God has promised that he is in the silence after the whirlwind. We know that God remembers us, when we can no longer speak his holy name.

I see no reason to assume that persons living with advanced dementia can no longer communicate with God, even when they can't speak to us. We know that God has promised that he is in the silence after the whirlwind. We know that God remembers us, when we can no longer speak his holy name. Our spiritual journey is not over when words fail.

I recently watched a moving video of Naomi Feil, who practices validation therapy, communicating with a person who could no longer speak. Feil, who is Jewish, gently sang "Jesus Loves Me" to Gladys Wilson, an African American woman. As Feil sang, Ms. Wilson first cried, then began to tap out the song, showing through repetitive movement that she was responding to the song.[2] This old woman, who sat for hours and days alone, suddenly had a friend, someone who met her as she was. Religious music was the medium to join these two, Jew and Christian, in a powerful moment. "There's a need there," Naomi Feil teaches us passionately. Indeed, there is, and it is precisely this unmet need that the psalmist described, a need for human and divine connection that is universal and timeless.

In the midst of death, we long for the gift of life. Thank God for Elenore, Sam and Sally, Naomi Feil, and all of you who are caregivers. You embody the presence of a living, caring God, and your devotion breaks through the sadness and darkness of dementia with a love that heals, accompanies, and enlivens.

3

I Know These People Mean Well: Dignity and Congregations

I BELIEVE that Sam, Sally, Elenore, and all caregivers—family and professional, those who care in their homes and those who care at a distance—are most resilient when they have a dependable circle of supportive people to rely on. The concern of friends and congregations does not take away the challenges of caregiving, but it facilitates the strength and courage caregiving demands.

Bonnie is a forty-year-old woman who has been, for more than twenty years, a companion and caregiver for persons with dementia and other chronic conditions. She works primarily in private homes, but also at times in long-term care facilities, filling in when family members are ill or out of town. I met Bonnie through Elenore, who told me, "I couldn't have done this without Bonnie. She is amazing!" Bonnie explained to me during our interview that she began this work after caring for her own grandmother. She realized that she had gifts for accompanying folks who were very ill, especially those with memory problems. An active member of her local Baptist congregation, she spoke repeatedly of her faith and the importance of "the Lord's help" in her life.

I was delighted to hear that Bonnie has experienced support and affirmation from her congregation. During a Sunday morning service, her pastor held her up to exemplify what it means to care for one another. What a marvelous venue for teaching how to show love within a congregation, and what a mountaintop experience for Bonnie. I am sure she left worship that day with all the dignity and inspiration she needed to get back to work, to continue with her ministry of care.

When was the last time that your congregation intentionally celebrated the ministry of someone who gives care? There is a tremendous need, for few caregivers receive what they need in the larger community. Recently I spoke to a group of psychiatrists about dementia care. A doctor in the group approached me afterward to mention that, in caring for her autistic child, she faces many of the same issues, including a need for dignity and grace. She has not found much support outside of her family, she told me. In smaller churches, dementia care could be part of a larger effort to support all caregivers, who have much in common. In larger congregations, dementia care could be given special attention, including affirmation of those, like Bonnie, who have been faithful caregivers for many years, and staff persons such as parish nurses, who can accompany caregivers.

Bonnie's story was a glimpse into one of the many ways a spiritual community can make a difference in the lives of some of God's humble and important servants (see my suggestions below). But the picture of what is currently going on in congregations is more complex. Kathy, a caregiver whose mother lives with Alzheimer's disease, had a less encouraging story about her faith community.

> How do I feel about the support from my congregation? To tell the truth, I'm not sure. I know the people here mean well. I just feel out of place sometimes, especially when I bring my mother along [to worship on Sundays]. They basically ignore us when she's with me—maybe we get a smile or two, but that's it. They used to try to talk with her, but they don't now.

My conversation with Kathy did not end with this interview. Several days later, she surprised me by calling me at home. (I gave all interview participants my number in case they had any questions.) She said, "I've been thinking about our interview, and I really *do* get support from my congregation. I wish I had said that in the interview."

Kathy's ambiguity about her church family became as interesting to me as anything we talked about face to face. I couldn't help wondering what was really going on. Did the truth simply slip out and then later cause Kathy to feel guilty? She clearly had some positive feelings about her congregation but was less sure how she felt about her mother's welcome. I suspect she is not the only caregiver with these conflicted feelings.

Perhaps Kathy's feelings are not surprising, since many congregations, although meaning well, do not know how to consistently extend hospitality to persons living with dementia. They may show sympathy for caregivers or for the person with dementia but fail to engage them with genuine empathy and sensitive respect. Persons with cognitive problems are viewed by some congregational members as radically different, which leads, in spatial terms (see chapter 2), to these members' visualizing the person with dementia as beneath them (as an object of care) rather than beside them (as a friend and companion). I suspect that Kathy sensed this and thus felt out of place, on behalf of her mother.

Sadly, this failure to welcome others is often practiced by older members of a congregation, not only by the young. These well-meaning Christians may try, once or twice, to respond to a person living with dementia, such as Kathy's mother, but then stop after their efforts appear to fall flat. Too often the unique needs of each person and her caregiver are not what guide their actions, even though they are motivated, in a general way, to embody Christ's love. Some people's tone of voice changes in their social interactions with persons living with dementia. As a nursing-home chaplain, I was horrified to hear visitors speaking to residents with a patronizing, overly sweet tone of voice, as though they were young children. (I would never speak to children in that tone either!) What can we do, as either personal or professional caregivers, to increase hospitality and respect for persons with impaired memories and

What can we do, as either personal or professional caregivers, to increase hospitality and respect for persons with impaired memories and their caregivers?

their caregivers? Are there tangible and attitudinal approaches that help? Should change begin with the congregation?

Congregations, Hospitality, and Caregiving

First, we face the question, Why should faith organizations be interested in health concerns? Aren't there enough other community organizations that can provide the resources and support that is needed? Why should congregations become distracted from preaching the gospel and presiding over the sacraments to focus on the needs of caregivers and those living with dementia?

There are indeed places to turn beyond the congregation, as I suggested to Sam and Sally when I recommended they call the Alzheimer's Association. I am encouraged by and excited about the growth of organizations where creative work is being done with both memory-impaired persons and their caregivers (see chapter 6). It is important for congregations to learn about the best of these and to partner with them whenever possible and appropriate.

I believe, however, that the church has a biblical, historic, and theological imperative to be the first line of support for its members (and, when possible, those in the larger community) who have health concerns, including dementia. Since they are dependent on the care of others, we also include their caregivers as part of our mission. We can begin with the commandment, "Honor your father and mother, so that your days may be long in the land that the Lord your God is giving you" (Exod 20:12). Because many persons with dementia and their caregivers are older adults, we are called to respond to their needs as part of the honor, respect, and special care we are commanded to show to all older persons in our families. I think it is no coincidence that the commandment instructing us to honor our parents is the only commandment with an attached promise—"That your days may be long . . ." In the New Testament as well there are instructions regarding elders. Timothy has stern words for those who do not attend to the needs of older persons, calling them "worse than an unbeliever" (1 Tim 5:8). Jesus modeled care for his mother, even from the cross, requesting that his friend take care of her after he death.

Tradition also suggests an important connection between faith communities and health ministries. The very word *hospital* evokes *hospitality* for those in need. Many hospitals in the United States have religious origins. The entire tradition of chaplaincy is another location where the cooperation and shared resources of religious groups and health organizations are obvious, along with the many health-care volunteers working with both religious and community-health sponsorship.

Our theology, specifically our understanding of discipleship, also points us to the importance of this ministry of support. Ours is a costly discipleship that sends us into the world, not into some sort of holy seclusion from the world's needs.[1] Thus, we are called to do what we can for our caregiving members, including those like Sam and Sally, as part of our larger calling as disciples.

> As the body of Christ, we have a responsibility to use our differing gifts to reach out with love and hospitality to those members who are serving year after year, as well as the persons they care for.

Of course, we are all different, and no one can be all things to all people. As the body of Christ, we have a responsibility to use our differing gifts to reach out with love and hospitality to those members who are serving year after year, as well as the persons they care for. As the apostle Paul wrote, "There are varieties of service, but the same Lord; and there are varieties of activities, but it is the same God who activates all of them in everyone" (1 Cor 12:5–6). Not everyone can visit, not everyone can preach, not everyone can cook casseroles—but everyone can find some way to extend love and care through the Lord who activates us all.

In the Lutheran church, we have a saying: "God's work; our hands." But are Christian congregations consistently available for persons with dementia and their caregivers? Are we joining together, using our varied gifts, to be the hands of God? My interviews with Bonnie and Kathy (above) suggest mixed results. I believe it is time for a reevaluation of our older-adult ministries in general, and ministry to caregivers in particular.

Through the years, I have been fortunate to meet a variety of persons who are passionate about congregational care with older adults. I would sometimes be invited to speak about older-adult ministry at a congregation only to discover that I learned from them as much as I shared. Parish nurses, pastors and other leaders were already creating exciting programs that offered both hospitality and support to older persons. Often, I would invite these leaders to come to Luther Seminary, where I taught pastoral care, to speak of their work. What an inspiration they were to me and to my students.

Like these leaders, I believe passionately that the days of the pastor who does everything—including giving all the pastoral care— are over. In today's busy world, we need to train and empower congregational leaders who will not only supplement but, in many cases, be the primary caregiver for those who have either a crisis (such as a family problem, death, or a sudden illness) or a long-term need (such as caregiving for someone with dementia). Often congregational leaders have a strong sense of vocation and are called to work with older adults as their primary mission.

What might your congregation do to be more helpful to you and to other caregivers? How can we as a church be more supportive and hospitable? Each congregation is different and has differing needs. One community may have rich resources for group support, including an accessible physical facility and a well-equipped staff, while another has an informal network for spiritual support. Still another congregation may see a need to change the ways they greet people on Sunday mornings to be sure that persons like Kathy's mother are not ignored. All congregations, however, can take some concrete steps to build on what already exists and to reform what needs changing. For the sake of simplicity, I offer below four possibilities (P's) for intentional congregational hospitality. But first, we need to focus on one word: listen!

When teaching seminary courses on aging ministry, I always began with the importance of listening before acting. "What is it that these older adults need?" must go before, "This is what we will try to implement." This deep listening is part of an overall commitment to being proactive, rather than reactive, in congregational care. In my own parish work, I found that most older adults are not shy about telling us what they need and want—if we ask! Too often, however, programs are created because a well-meaning leader decides what is needed. News flash, pastors and other congregational leaders: what we learned in seminary or read in our favorite book may not fit the needs and resources of your congregation. We must listen first. Calling on older members who have been around the church for many years is a great way to begin.

We listen to discover precisely what caregivers who are accompanying someone experiencing dementia are struggling with, and what resources they already have. The answers may surprise you. I must confess that I learned the importance of listening after I first failed. As a nursing-home chaplain, I started a support group for caregivers (largely in response to a request from my administrator, who had an alternative motive: he thought it would cut down on family complaints to him!). For a few weeks, I had four or five loyal participants, until someone in the group told me, "Chaplain Ramsey, we appreciate your efforts, and we are coming to the group to support you. But the truth is, we already have a support group! It is the gang that meets in the lobby everyday just before dinner time. We've been doing that for years!" Next time I considered a new program, I listened first.

If you are a professional caregiver, listening is a first step. But after listening, the question remains—what do caregivers of folks with dementia, and those who are memory impaired, need from their faith community? Here we must proceed with humility and caution, because of the variety in congregations, in both needs and resources. But there are responses that are universal and can be easily adapted to your setting—mainly, prayer, preparation, presence (which may include practical assistance), and partnership.

> We listen to discover precisely what caregivers who are accompanying someone experiencing dementia are struggling with, and what resources they already have. The answers may surprise you.

Four Possibilities for Congregational Care

1. Prayer (during worship, by visitors and by those they visit, with prayer partners)

2. Preparation (education, leadership, bringing everyone on board)

3. Presence and practical help (visits by trained congregational caregivers; assistance from anyone with special skills and time)

4. Partnership (with leaders from already successful community organizations)

Prayer

I have often wondered why it is our practice, in most Christian churches, to pray only for someone when they are in the middle of a crisis. Perhaps religious communities have been affected by the dramatic-news-cycle approach, where the latest crisis draws attention, only to be forgotten when the next crisis arises. Why not also pray for those dealing with long-term challenges? What might happen if we regularly held up caregivers and asked God to be with them with their daily tasks—with work that often lasts for years? Of course, not all caregivers want to be named publicly—so this is another place where listening and asking must precede acting.

Prayer is a ministry by as well as for older adults. The prayers of Christians who are busy professionals can be joined by the prayers of those who are now homebound, including those with mild cognitive impairment and their caregivers. We don't need to simply pray for those with special needs; we need to invite them to pray for us. If you ask a person you are visiting to pray for you, you will demonstrate that she isn't the only vulnerable and needy one and that you value her prayer ministry.

I also think that pastors, parish nurses, Stephen ministers, and all others who visit caregivers and persons with dementia at home should pray during each visit. Surprisingly, people tell me that this is not always the case. I do ask the people I visit for permission to pray, but I have never had someone say "no." Asking what the caregiver

> We don't need to simply pray for those with special needs; we need to invite them to pray for us.

would like us to pray for is often a powerful way to bring daily challenges to God and simultaneously educate ourselves on that person's greatest needs. In some cases, the persons you are visiting may wish to add petitions to your prayer; at other times, they prefer you to do the praying for them. Don't forget to invite the person living with dementia to join in as well, when possible.

I learned about the importance of a prayer ministry by older adults when I conducted interviews for a book on aging and spiritual resiliency. One respondent, Rebecca, was not only homebound but could not get up from her reclining chair without assistance. When I asked her how she filled her days, she told me, "Well, lately, we've had a lot in trouble in our congregation. Some died, and some have been real sick. So, you have to pray for everybody, every day. You don't just pray one time and quit. You pray for your family. You pray for the overall church."[2] Later, as I left, she added, "And now I'll have to pray for you, Pastor Jan!"

I think setting up intentional prayer partners can also be a powerful form of support and hospitality. This is especially helpful when caregiving goes on a long time, as it does with dementia care. Prayer partnerships often increase intimacy among members, even as they extend support from God and from the congregation. Prayer partners should, of course, be chosen carefully. They can be suggested by a congregational leader or by the people who already know one another (so don't over-organize). Linking two caregivers can be especially helpful.

Preparation

So much fear (and the avoidance that follows) is mitigated by basic education and preparation. Christian education that begins with Scripture is built on solid ground. For example, congregational leaders can teach that nowhere in Christian Scripture or doctrine is it written that we stop being God's precious children because we develop a disability. On the contrary, all members have a special honor and a unique purpose, as Paul so elegantly wrote. Rather, the love and acceptance of the One who is at the center of our life together is put into action by welcoming the most vulnerable, such as those experiencing dementia and their caregivers.

Sunday programs during the education hour, comments during the sermon, pamphlets sent out or placed in the pews, special guest speakers with expertise in dementia care—these are just a few of the possible venues for congregational education. I would suggest including someone who has expertise in communicating with persons with dementia (see chapter 2) since this is an area of such importance for member-to-member interactions.

It is also important for congregational leaders to have knowledge of local (and web) resources when visiting persons with dementia and their caregivers. As my visit with Sam and Sally showed, not everyone is aware of local and national organizations that exist to help. Online support groups, for example, can be perfect for persons who are at home most days.

Presence and Practical Help

The best way to avoid having someone feel forgotten is to call, visit, or send cards to them regularly. It matters who comes, how often they come, and how supportive they are—but mostly, it matters that someone reaches out. Many people I've met do not expect the pastor to visit often, but without at least a visit a year, they feel disappointed, no matter how many other congregational caregivers come. This inclination is not ideal, but it is simply true—there is something unique about a pastoral visit when Christians are hurting, lonely, and in need.

Stephen Ministers and parish nurses, however, are not just fill-ins for a pastor but following their own vocations. They bring unique gifts and have special training that often make a tangible difference in the lives of caregivers. When congregations have an active ministry of lay caregivers, they inevitably have a closer congregation where people feel cared for and heard. They also help the larger congregation to keep those living with dementia and their caregivers in mind by advocating for their inclusion in all aspects

The love and acceptance of the One who is at the center of our life together is put into action by welcoming the most vulnerable.

of congregational life and modeling hospitality each time they are present with the larger membership.

When caregivers and persons with memory issues are at worship or other events, presence takes the form of greeting and actively responding to the person. When you can ask specifically about how a caregiver is doing, such as, "How did that visit to the doctor go last week?" or when you call a person with impaired memory by name, dignity is enhanced and people feel welcomed and included. This requires the discipline of paying attention to what others tell us, but it is easier than it seems. You don't have to remember everything (confessions here of a pastor and a pastoral counselor).

My research on spiritual resiliency and aging taught me that practical help contributes more than we might realize to feelings of being cared for and remembered. As one man in Germany who loved to help his neighbors told me, "Being a Christian belongs right in the middle of everyday life!"[3] One woman proudly told me that her friends at church come by frequently to help with household tasks. It is, however, important to remember that some people resist practical assistance. The capacity to receive help, as well as give it, can be difficult for persons who have been active all their lives. Some members of our congregations are still working on this aspect of spiritual development.

Caregivers and their care partners immediately get a feeling of welcome when practical concerns are obviously attended to.

Attending to practical concerns is important for creating an environment of welcome. Are the bathrooms accessible and easy to find? Are pavements cleared of ice and snow, and is it possible to safely drop off a person near the front door? Is transportation provided or arranged for when needed? Does the nave include shorter pews that create spaces where wheelchairs will fit? Caregivers and their care partners immediately get a feeling of welcome when such practical concerns are obviously attended to.

Just as with all of my suggestions, we must listen first and continue to listen. But no matter what you find to be the specific needs of you congregation, you can always trust this simple slogan: Show up!

Partnerships

No congregation should or could try to meet all the needs of its members. Fortunately, the recent vision of congregational care includes a strong emphasis on partnerships with other organizations, including secular not-for-profits. Like congregations, many not-for-profits want to be catalysts for community change. They share our values of hospitality, mutual respect, sharing resources, and caring for the most vulnerable among us. When congregations cooperate with secular nonprofits, they establish limited partnerships, which means that both partners agree to cooperate to work for justice and mercy in our communities, but they are legally limited in many ways. These limitations do not decrease the potential for good that can be done.

Of course, a great deal of planning, communicating, and discernment is called for when community organizations and churches (and synagogues and mosques) decide to form a focused partnership. It is important to be clear about finances, leadership, and even tax implications. Who will vet the volunteers, and who will be providing the space to meet and work? Do members of the groups feel competitive or cooperative? Your congregation and the community group may be excited about different goals, and for different reasons, so whose goals will be given priority?

Despite these challenges, it makes good sense to cooperate with community groups whenever possible. Especially in a time where government funding for social services have declined, congregations can join with not-for-profits to fill the gap. Throughout the United States, congregations and secular organizations are cooperating to address topics like partner abuse, poverty, and the needs of children, working together to challenge the emphasis on materialism and individualism today. Dementia care is one of many challenges facing communities where cooperation makes sense. In joining together, we not only increase our numbers of volunteers and our financial resources. We also learn skills and strategies from those in organizations with expertise and experience beyond our own.

Advocacy

Perhaps you are reading these ideas for congregational care and thinking, "Well, that sounds great, but I can't see it happening in my congregation." I am hoping, as spiritual communities become more aware of disrespectful sins of omission or commission, that caregivers themselves will become motivated to advocate for improved congregational ministries. I suspect that those persons who have been caregivers, like Elenore and Kathy, have the necessary wisdom and motivation to help congregations rethink their ministry approaches regarding persons who are memory impaired. Becoming an advocate for change can have two positive effects. Most importantly, caregivers can help congregations improve their attitudes and actions toward vulnerable church members. Second, advocacy can help caregivers themselves redirect some of their grief and frustration. I am reminded of the tremendous good that has been accomplished by groups such as Mothers Against Drunk Driving. Perhaps we need Caregivers Against Apathetic Congregations.

Challenges to Implementing the Possibilities

I was shocked, as a chaplain in a church-related care facility, to hear comments such as the following from my pastoral colleagues: "I know you don't see me around this place [a nursing home] much. It is just too depressing!" On so many levels, it was distressing to realize how professional leaders—seminary graduates—could be so unprepared for the demands of ministry. Did they think their vocation was all about having fun? I also lamented that they were so frightened of dementia and of aging itself, perhaps asking themselves, "Will I be lying there myself someday, dependent on the care of others?" And, finally, they were clearly uninformed about the importance of simply being present, even when those we minister to can no longer respond with words to our prayers and blessings. These distressing comments were a large part of what motivated me to return to graduate school and prepare to teach seminarians about aging.

> By forming partnerships we not only increase our numbers of volunteers and our financial resources. We also learn skills and strategies from those in organizations with expertise and experience beyond our own.

I continue to find distressing levels of apathy about aging ministries in general and dementia and caregiving specifically. Considering our demographics, this is beyond perplexing. I realize that even though Alzheimer's disease is now the sixth leading cause of death in older adults,[4] dementia is not a sexy topic. It is not one that many people are motivated to address—until, of course, it comes to them or to someone in their families. Like other communities, congregations prefer to focus on the young, the attractive, those with "potential." I suspect fear of dementia is part of a larger anxiety—fear of aging itself.

Aging is part of the normal life cycle, yet in our culture we work to avoid the realities of growing old. Unless we die young, we will all find ourselves, someday, the victim of the ageism we create today. Most of us will all someday become the people we are striving to avoid today—older, frailer, and in need of human community. Meanwhile, we need to get in touch with our own ageist attitudes as a first step in working toward creating dementia-friendly communities.

Ever since the prominent gerontologist (and first director of the National Institute on Aging) Robert Butler coined the term *ageism* (in 1969),[5] gerontologists have been able to identify and understand that stereotypes, myths, and disdain for older adults are similar, in some ways, to racism or sexism. If you have ever heard comments about older drivers, slower clerks in a department store, or women described as "old hags," you have witnessed everyday ageism. Often, this discrimination takes the form of simply being ignored. At other times, people can be over solicitous. Living in the South at seventy-two, I am frequently called "honey" by persons taking care of me in a variety of settings.

But my passion for fighting ageism has never left me. When I began teaching seminary in 2003, I found that many young students found studying and working with older adults to be a strange and disorienting experience—perhaps simply because they had so little contact with older persons. On the positive side, however, I also found that as they began to interact with older adults because of their class requirements, they increased their appreciation for the complexities, surprises, and nuances of being a congregational caregiver. They increased their appreciation for diversity among people of all ages. Best of all, they deepened their ideas of what makes us wise and valuable in a society that tends to value our economic production above all. Most surprising of all, they found that it was a relief to admit the limits of their own experience. They liked that they could feel more relaxed around older adults. To grow, my students needed to be open to their own limitations and to take to heart Paul's admonishment, "Guard against self-deception, each of you. If someone among you thinks he is wise in this age, let him become foolish so that he can become wise. For the wisdom of this age is foolishness with God" (1 Cor 3:18–19).

However, in a society such as the present-day United States, where knowledge is highly compartmentalized, it is difficult to adopt and maintain Paul's countercultural view of wisdom—that we must become foolish before becoming wise. Everywhere we look, including the media and even in institutions of higher learning, we see an emphasis on technical knowledge and defined stages of expertise. Even though we may agree with social scientists' view that human development is both cognitive and emotional, we are immersed in a culture where the cognitive is valued over all else. A countercultural option is to recognize that, as we grow older, we increase the possibility for a higher level of consciousness because our perspectives have expanded and we can maintain multiple points of view simultaneously.[6] This is precisely the wisdom we need to accompany those living with dementia, for whom emotions often become more important than factual content.

Getting Excited about Ministries with Older Adults

I believe congregations need to have deeper conversations about hospitality itself, teaching that welcoming means more than encouraging members to greet newcomers. It is easy to warmly

> A countercultural option is to recognize that, as we grow older, we increase the possibility for a higher level of consciousness because our perspectives have expanded and we can maintain multiple points of view simultaneously.

welcome people who are attractive, intelligent, and youthful, but we are called to extend hospitality for all, including those who are old, cognitively impaired, and frail.

It is not a distraction but a benefit—in fact a vocation—for congregations to become more hospitable. Working to welcome those who are living with dementia by proactively implementing ministries based on what is possible (see above) can strengthen congregations and challenge us where we need to be challenged—to be sensitive listeners and proactive planners. All congregations need to examine what we do, not only what we are writing in mission statements. We need to ask ourselves, repeatedly, "What stories are we creating about our own congregation? How are these stories creating us and shaping our life together?"

Fortunately, we have rich resources to guide us in congregational story writing. There are no shortages of healing stories in the Christian narrative to use as our anchors. Jesus obviously preferred to hang out with the poor, sick, and wounded—those who recognized their hunger. He had little patience for the strong, proud, and self-sufficient, who appeared not to need his message. Later, in the early church, the central rituals of the faithful, baptism and Holy Communion, were centered around the story of brokenness before resurrection. The words of these rituals reflect the narrative of a suffering Savior who died before being raised to glory. Christians are called to be a "vulnerable communion," not a club for the powerful, rich, and famous.

Thomas Reynolds, who is the parent of a son with disabilities, has written a book exploring the ways in which disability has been misunderstood theologically, for example as divine punishment or as inadequate faith—or even as some sort of special blessing. Based on a "cult of normalcy" we view those abnormal persons as persons to be shunned or pitied. Reynolds believes that acts based on pity, while intended to help the disabled, ironically deepen social exclusion and "stymies the genuine welcome."[7] On the other hand,

It is easy to warmly welcome people who are attractive, intelligent, and youthful, but we are called to extend hospitality for all, including those who are old, cognitively impaired, and frail.

in relationships of mutuality, both participants experience hospitality and increased sensitivity to human need. Writes Judith Jordan,

> In a mutual exchange, one is both affecting the other and being affected by the other; one extends oneself out to the other and is also receptive to the impact of the other. There is openness to influence, emotional availability, and a constantly changing pattern of responding to and affecting the other's state.[8]

We can be grateful that those living with dementia and their caregivers remind us of this shared humanity and common need. They remind us that all who hunger and thirst after righteousness are welcome at the Lord's table. They remind us that all the baptized, who are marked with the cross of Christ forever, are his beloved children. In other words, they remind us of the invitation that says, "If you are hurt, confused, and frail, please come join us, for so are we all."

Christians believe that at baptism we are given more than a name; we receive the gift of dignity. When a person is baptized, the congregation present renews its promise to welcome the new member. Asks the celebrant at an Episcopalian baptism, for example, "Will you strive for justice and peace among all people, and respect the dignity of every human being?" The people respond, "I will, with God's help."[9] Thus, for Christians, dignity is communal, lasting, and gracious, given to the newly baptized as a gift. We know that we are "sealed by the Holy Spirit in Baptism and marked as Christ's own forever."[10] We are welcomed into the family as members of the body of Christ—a family that has promised to respect the dignity of us all.

Reflection on Psalm 8

O Lord, our Lord,
    how great is your name throughout the earth!
    And your glory in the heavens above.
    Even the mouths of children and infants
    exalt your glory in front of your foes
    and put to shame enemies and rebels.
When I observe the heavens,
    the work of your hands,
    the moon and the stars you set in their place—
    what is the mortal that you be mindful of him,
    the son of man, that you should care for him?
Yet you made him a little lower than the angels;
    you have crowned him with glory and honor.
    You made him rule over the works of your hands;
    you have put all things under his feet—
    sheep and oxen without number
    and even the beasts of the field,
    the birds of the air, the fish of the sea,
    and all that swim the paths of the ocean.
O Lord, our Lord,
    how great is your name all over the earth!

WE ARE crowned with "glory and honor." What a marvelous way to imagine the dignity that is ours from God. I picture the psalmist lying in a pasture surrounded by the "beasts of the field" and gazing at the heavens on a clear night. He thinks not of the work he did that day, nor of the tasks waiting him on the next, but of the greatness of God. "Lord, I can't believe you gave human beings a second thought, in light of all this majesty," he ponders. "Yet, you not only think of us, but you care for us! And you honored us with a status 'a little lower than the angels' and made us your designated caregivers! We are responsible for 'all things,' all the works of your hands. We are called to praise your name 'all over the earth.'"

When was the last time you were able to get away from it all, on a beautiful night, to gaze at the heavens, the moon, and the stars? When were you last alone—or, rather, when were you last able to get some quality one-on-one time with God? Even though God accompanies you each day as you attend to the details that need your attention, it is important to escape from it all at times. Just as a couple needs time away from domestic responsibilities, to listen to each other and to be heard by each other, so in our intimate relationship with God, we need these times apart. Even when we are too tired to form words of prayer, we are renewed by simply being open to the presence of the One who loves us most.

When we leave behind, for a time, the noises of everyday existence, we are often able to enlarge our perspective and reimagine how we fit into God's creation. Surrounded by the natural world, and away from our responsibilities, we can't help but marvel at all that God has made—including us! What a contrast between our smallness and our importance as God's chosen disciples. What an honor to care for each other as God cares for us!

Several details in this psalm delight me, such as the psalmist's suggestion that "infants" join in praising God. Clearly, the writer of these words did not see intellectual ability as a prerequisite for glorifying God. These infants, who do not yet have the ability to form words, can still join in the music of the spheres. These words suggest that those at the opposite end of the life cycle, who may once again find themselves unable to form words, are equally a part of the chorus of praise. Young infants in their cradles and old persons in a care facility are just as important as the voices of the

> Even when we are too tired to form words of prayer, we are renewed by simply being open to the presence of the One who loves us most.

Mormon Tabernacle Choir when it comes to membership in God's holy choir.

Another thing I appreciate is that the psalmist never names his enemy. Just as the apostle Paul never explains his thorn in the flesh, so the psalmist leaves it wide open for us to imagine who or what the enemy may be. An army? A jealous tribe? Drought or floods? Or maybe illness, in himself or his (or her) family? We never learn the details, and this makes it easier for us to identify with the psalmist's cry for help and with his gratitude that God is not only his Creator but also his Caregiver. He puts his trust in God. He separates himself from the enemy and sees himself in partnership with God. God's victory become his victory. Praise for God becomes the only conceivable response.

The psalmist has his own questions, just we often do. But when he asks, "What is man?" he doesn't identify reasoning, physical strength, or material productivity as the factors that ensure his dignity. Rather, human beings take a place, albeit an honored one, simply as part of the rest of creation, as part of God's created order. Our place in God's beloved creation is the source of our dignity. In relationship with God, the psalmist sees how he fits into the universe, and he is filled with awe.

> As we recognize our humble place in the universe, and as we acknowledge the honor and responsibility we have been given, we marvel at the contrast between our smallness under the heavens and the glory and honor God ascribes to us.

Dignity in this psalm is a gift from God, and it is also a way to live. As we recognize our humble place in the universe, and as we acknowledge the honor and responsibility we have been given, we marvel at the contrast between our smallness under the heavens and the glory and honor God ascribes to us. The psalmist sees this as natural and inevitable—because we are made by God and kept in God's care, we can accept our responsibilities on this earth.

When we care for someone with dementia, we are caring for a part of the beautiful world that God made. We are participating in an important role that is both humble and important. We are filling one little corner of the universe with devotion and love, yet we are cared for by God as though we and our loved one were the whole show.

We need continual renewal to remain faithful to the work of caregiving. The beauty of nature—not only the moon and the stars, but the sounds of a symphony or the look on a small child's face—these are among the resources all around us, free of charge and readily available. We can start by getting away from our TVs and computers to get out into the night. Gaze at the night sky and be filled with wonder. We can leave the little rooms of our lives and get out into God's big room. As we do so, whatever has been going on that day often shifts dramatically, and we are taken to a different place—still a beautiful part of the world but no longer at center stage. Oh, Lord, how great is your name in all the world!

Part Two

Grace

Introduction

I Try to Give Him Choices: Grace in Everyday Life

AMY IS a home caregiver for her husband, Jeff, who has early Alzheimer's disease. In an interview, she told me about an exchange the couple had:

> Jeff told me the other day, "When this memory problem gets worse, I hope I will still be in charge of my own life. I don't want to be led around like a helpless child. I am still a man!" I know that scares him, being dependent on me, so I try to give him choices when I can. Just ordinary things, like chocolate or vanilla ice cream for dessert.

Amy understands herself as an ordinary caregiver with no expertise, but in these few words we see the love she has for her husband. Because she cares for him, she wants him to retain a sense of dignity, as we explored in part 1. She not only hears but listens to him. She listens to his deep need to feel like "a man," in charge of his own life. There are increasing limits to his autonomy every day, and Amy recognizes the pain this is causing him. She views caregiving as going beyond meeting his physical needs; she wants to make his life as fulfilling as possible.

Amy mentioned several other "small things" she does to help Jeff retain as much dignity as possible. She always puts out two shirts on the bed in the morning and asks him to choose one. She asks him to help with household chores and checks with him before making plans to have someone come visit them. She also makes sure that he is present when the doctor talks to her about his condition. "I won't talk about him behind his back. I wouldn't want someone to do that to me!"

I admire Amy for her efforts to maintain Jeff's self-respect. I also realize that no close relationship, including Amy and Jeff's, is perfect. None of us are consistently patient with and sensitive to the needs of the person for whom we care. As one of the women I interviewed put it, quite simply, "I am so tired of losing my cool with him, and he doesn't make matters any easier by refusing to cooperate (with dressing, etc.)." Those with memory problems have challenges too, and are sometimes tempted to blame caregivers for life's frustrations. All of us can lose our patience, act out of anger or fear, or simply ignore the needs of the other. In Christian language, we are simultaneously sinners and saints, and that doesn't end simply because an illness is now present. Nowhere is the messy combination of love and irritation more obvious than in our intimate family relationships, where so much is at stake and where we turn to meet so many of our emotional needs.

Our relationship histories complicate the best of efforts to be patient and sensitive. Later in this same interview, Amy told me that she and her husband have not always had an easy time in their marriage. When they were new parents, Jeff often traveled out of town for his job and worked extremely long hours. He was rarely available to the family, and Amy felt like a single parent, struggling to meet the challenges of parenting, including caring for a special-needs child. She acknowledges, "We worked that through in some counseling, and now he realizes how hard it was for me much of the time."

Amy's forgiveness of Jeff is as important in their current partnership as her love for him. Forgiveness diminishes the anger, resentment, and disappointment that can slowly eat at a relationship that is not based on forgiveness. Fortunately, Amy's love and forgiveness have freed her—not to be a perfect caregiver but to be more sensitive to Jeff and to find ways to empower him through "just ordinary

All of us can lose our patience, act out of anger or fear, or simply ignore the needs of the other. In Christian language, we are simultaneously sinners and saints, and that doesn't end simply because an illness is now present.

> What I hope for are dignity and grace.
>
> —Lorna

things." Amy and Jeff's partnership reflects not only dignity but grace.

Grace: Dignity's Partner in Hope

Early in this book, I introduced you to Lorna, who gave me the words that inspired the title of this book. In part 1, I explored what dignity might have to do with the experience of living with memory impairments and with caregiving. My vision of dignity as relational, as something we live, was deepened as I reflected on the wisdom of the caregivers like Elenore who have come to see relationships built on dignity as forms of accompaniment.

But Lorna did not speak only of dignity. Important as it is, a dignified relationship is cold soup without a second ingredient—the warmth of grace. Even when we feel respected, we long for graceful, loving relationships—the daily nurture that we need all through our lives. Human experience, along with psychological research, has revealed that a healthy, happy life is one that is rooted in gracious relationships (what we give each other freely) rather than in exchanges based on careful calculations (what we think we owe each other).

When I asked Lorna what she meant by dignity and grace, she chose not to be more specific and just repeated the two words quietly. Perhaps that is because both grace and dignity are such complex and vivid experiences that Lorna did not want to trivialize them with a quick summary. I believe it is important to respect the richness of these words, but I also have found that unpacking them gives us insights into the ways caregiving can become more spiritually resilient.

The term *grace* has a long history and carries meanings that differ according to context and individual experiences. Like a multifaceted diamond, grace shines with the varied light it reflects. Looking at the words and actions of caregivers like Amy and Lorna, the word *grace* can guide us to understand more deeply how God is working with us to be God's disciples in a hurting, broken world.

To some people, grace is linked with visible beauty. We speak of the gracefulness of a dancer who moves with elegance. For others, grace means gratitude. We "say grace" at the dinner table to thank God for our blessings. We also speak, often humorously, of gracing another with our presence and about having the grace to withdraw from a bad situation.[1] In these understandings, there is a consistent theme: grace is an undeserved gift. Perhaps what is beautiful and what we are most grateful for must first be recognized as gifts we do not deserve.

A well-read and intelligent person like Lorna would be aware, on some level, of many different meanings for the word grace, but perhaps she is hoping for grace particularly within the relationships her mother has with those who care for her. Now living in a full-care facility, her mother is dependent on both the obvious and the subtle forms of graciousness from those who attend to her most intimate needs. Will they be loving and forgiving? Will they have the sensitivity to give her mother choices whenever possible, or will they communicate wordlessly, simply with an irritated tone of voice, that she is a tiresome burden? Lorna is hoping they will be gracious.

A person of faith, Lorna is most likely thinking of her mother's relationship with God, who loves and forgives us at any life stage or condition. She no doubt wishes for God's graceful presence, a presence so necessary in the untidy world of dementia and caregiving. Any Christian caregiver knows that God's grace is found not in some lofty remote sphere but rather amid everyday life, where we must carefully watch and listen for it.

Hearing Lorna's words convinced me that to wish for grace is to wish for the most precious aspect of our relationship with God. Like dignity, grace is not a thing, and we do not experience grace in isolation from others. Rather, grace is relational, something we find as we live our lives. Grace is a way to be in the world, a way to respond to God. Above all, for Christians, grace is the freely given and totally undeserved love we see on the cross. Here is grace in

> Grace is a way to be in the world, a way to respond to God. Above all, for Christians, grace is the freely given and totally undeserved love we see on the cross.

action, love with the highest cost, love that leads to new life and forgiveness.

Grace as Love and Forgiveness

The people I've taught and counseled, my readings in the social sciences, and my own caregiving experiences have convinced me that we human beings need to experience love each day of our lives. On days when human love is not available, we need to draw upon the reservoir of love we have stored up in our hearts through the years, love we experienced in relationships with the most important people in our lives and with God.

We also need to experience, over and over, both forgiveness for our own shortcomings and the capacity to forgive others. Although physical and emotional healing cannot be neatly separated, forgiveness is often as important to us as physical healing.[2] Forgiveness is a lifestyle, a way to move on from resentment and the desire for revenge into a future filled with the possibility of fresh connections with others. Because we forgive and are forgiven, the past becomes less tragic, the present becomes more bearable, and future relationships no longer fill us with anxiety.

Along with dignity, the gracious gifts of love and forgiveness empower us to get on the train (see chapter 2) and accompany one another in all of life's journeys, including caregiving and life with dementia. Love and forgiveness unlock the past, present, and future. Through these gifts, we get glimpses of joy in our past stories and are unstuck from past mistakes, both our own and those of others. Only in the presence of love and forgiveness can we welcome the present day as a fresh adventure, and only love and forgiveness have the power to allow us to believe that the future will be not only tolerable but promising. Love and forgiveness are most important at times of crisis and ongoing difficulties. They enable us to make meaning out of even the most extreme suffering. Both our ability to hope and our sense of self-efficacy ("I think I can!") depend on the ability to love and forgive ourselves and others.

Forgiveness is a lifestyle, a way to move on from resentment and the desire for revenge into a future filled with the possibility of fresh connections with others.

Amy's sensitivity to her husband is one example of the gift of respect. Dignity is something we live out in our relationships, but respect is a gift we grant each other. For the casual listener, Amy's words about ice-cream flavors sound as though she is simply trying to find ways to get through the day. But love and forgiveness are present as well, as they often are, in the "little things" of their everyday lives. Their relationship is flourishing because Jeff is less likely to see his partner as robbing him of personal freedom.

I believe that a life committed to love and forgiveness has an additional benefit—a wiser perspective. These gracious ways to be in the world keep us focused on what matters most and help us appreciate the little gifts we give and receive from each other, at ordinary moments. Even on days when we are surrounded by ugliness, cruelty, resentment, and fear, grace can suddenly appear to show us something precious. Grace points to the beauty of our mortal existence and teaches us what to treasure most.

> Dignity is something we live out in our relationships, but respect is a gift we grant each other.

Challenges to Grace in the Presence of Dementia

As Jeff's dementia progresses, he and Amy will face additional challenges to their relationship. It is never easy to live with grace in our intimate relationships—parent and child, partner to partner, friend and friend—even without the presence of dementia. But when dementia comes along and tries to derail us from living with a vision of grace, we need increased insight, empathy, and maturity. Happily, God grants us the strength and wisdom we need to discern and respond to what we are up against. Jesus's teachings show us what love and forgiveness look like, and the Holy Spirit helps us imagine a world where love and forgiveness reign. The Bible calls this world the kingdom of God, and I believe it is a world of grace.

4

What's Love Got to Do with It?
Grace and Love

WHEN BONNIE (see also chapter 3) first told her family that she was considering taking a job as a caregiver for people with dementia, she got mixed reactions. Her sisters approved and encouraged her, but her cousin, who was already working as a caregiver, told Bonnie, "Don't get too close to them [those with dementia]. You have to think of yourself first, and it is hard to see them decline and die." Bonnie told me she often thinks about that warning, but has decided to ignore it. "I can't do this without love," she told me. "Love is what keeps me going."

Bonnie's cousin was concerned about the cost of love—the grief that comes when we allow ourselves to care deeply and risk the pain of loss. I understand her fears. During my years as a nursing-home chaplain, there was a large part of me that was constantly grieving. I would sometimes confess to my husband that I was tired of running into people in the grocery store who would break into tears when they saw me, saying, "Oh, you did my mother's funeral!" I loved my job, but it is not easy to care for very frail older adults, including those with dementia. Boundaries must be kept, and we must find an adequate path to self-care. But I also agree with Bonnie—without love, giving care in the presence of dementia is just hard, depressing work. Who would want to do that?

Bonnie's love for the persons she cares for introduces us to the close relationship between care and love. The overlap between these terms is an important one and may be disguised, in part, because of our own language. Doing research for this book, I discovered an interesting bit of diversity in terminology. In the United Kingdom (and perhaps elsewhere), the term *caregiver* is not often used. Rather, a person who accompanies someone with illness or disabilities is referred to as a *carer*. At first this sounded awkward to me, but as I considered the word, I decided I liked it very much. To be a caregiver implies we, as subjects, are giving something, namely care, to an object. But a carer is part of a dynamic team, with two subjects. This term also opens more space to consider who is caring for whom. (How often do we say, "I'm getting more out of this than I'm giving!") *Carer* works for me, especially since we do not describe ourselves as *love givers* but as *lovers*.

A person can certainly take up the work of caregiving without love, either for a family member or as a paid professional, but love is central to *gracious* caregiving. This is not to say that any of us are consistently carers, or lovers. We remain sinners and saints in this work, as in any other. Some of us have to struggle to love. I have met caregivers who appeared to be largely motivated by greed, guilt, or social pressure. (Small wonder that elder abuse remains so prevalent.)

Happily, however, I have been amazed repeatedly by the love shown by most caregivers. Some offer care in their own homes (like Sam and Sally), some care at a distance (as I did), and some live nearby and visit often (as did Lorna and Elenore). The women and men I sat with as a parish pastor, those I counseled as a family therapist, and those I interviewed for this book are all carers/lovers who amaze me with their patience, devotion, and compassion. It is a tough, realistic love they feel and show—they experience impatience, fatigue, and even sometimes a secret wish, when suffering is great, that their loved one will come to an end more quickly. They do not always find it easy to be loving, day after day, year after year, but they have discovered that gracious caregiving is something they can choose to do. They make the choice to love.

> We do not describe ourselves as *love givers* but as *lovers*.

What's Love Got to Do with Dementia Care?

But what do I mean when I say they decide to love? Love is a word people use carelessly. Sometimes, as a marriage therapist, I wished we had more words to use to describe love, like the Inuit, who have over fifty words for snow.[1] We are stuck with one word to cover a wide range of meanings and contexts. We may say, "I love chocolate," or "I love the way I feel with you." Often when we say, "I love you," we are typically referring to a feeling of constant affection for someone else,[2] but do we really want to limit love to a feeling? I agree with Rabbi David Wolpe that love is better viewed not simply as a feeling but as "*an enacted emotion*. To love is to feel and act lovingly."[3]

But even if we accept Rabbi Wolpe's understanding, that only moves the problem of defining love back a bit, because we must still describe what kinds of feelings and actions are part of love, including when we are referring to love in the presence of dementia. What, if anything, does love as a feeling/action have to do with caregiving for someone? Or with being diagnosed with dementia yourself? It would be easy to be totally confused and overwhelmed by the multiple meanings of love in our culture, but, as a Christian, I prefer to begin with the greatest love story of all time, the word of God.

The Bible gives us a complicated, colorful, and powerful picture of enacted love. The word for love most often used in the New Testament is *agape*. This love is understood as selfless care for others or good will toward others. In contrast to *eros* (sexual love) and *philos* (brotherly love), *agape* is the love revealed in Jesus Christ. I believe that *agape* is closest to what we mean when we speak of the love of selfless caregiving. It is the love that motivates persons like Bonnie and inspires many of us to serve wherever we see a need. This love, however, is not given in the abstract. Biblical love is enacted in specific situations. In Genesis, we read about God's creation of the world—freely, and only because God wanted to create. I always think of this creation moment when I hear the lyrics

Love is better viewed not simply as a feeling but as "*an enacted emotion*. To love is to feel and act lovingly."

"making love out of nothing at all."[4] God's love is visible, too, in the stories of flawed heroes like David, who were given opportunities to serve and lead even though they made dreadful mistakes. And it had to be God's love in action when he sent prophets who seemed half crazy, like Elisha and Ezekiel, to keep the Jews away from false gods and to urge them back on the path of justice and mercy.

And then, in part 2 of Scripture, the New Testament, God's love is embodied in its ultimate form. We read in the world's favorite Bible verse, John 3:16, that "God so loved the world . . ." This is the chapter where we learn that God was fed up with watching human beings treat each other without love or justice. God's answer was to send Jesus to be a model of perfect love and, on the cross, to enact love as no one had done before or will ever do again. Jesus raised the bar for enacting love and he had the perfect right to command us to love one another in response (John 13:24). Secular definitions of love pale beside this picture of divine love. In the midst of the complicated life of dementia care, thinking of Jesus is the best way to ponder enacted love.

> In the midst of the complicated life of dementia care, thinking of Jesus is the best way to ponder enacted love.

Love for the Outcasts

The image of Jesus healing the sick is a Christian classic, but we don't always consider just whom he was healing (the outcasts and sinners) or what rules he was breaking when he did so (Jewish rules against becoming unclean or working on the Sabbath). It is interesting that he was particularly moved to heal the lepers. We have numerous references to these healings (Matt 8:3, 10:8; Luke 4:27, 17:14). Why did this small-town rabbi show his tangible love for the very persons others in his society not only feared but rejected? Clearly, for Jesus, love is a seamless combination of feelings (of compassion) and action (of healing).

Is dementia the new leprosy? Because we are so obsessed with cognitive functioning, because we are so sure that we can be expert problem solvers if only we know enough about science and technology, we contemporary Americans often reject and even despise whatever reminds us of our intellectual vulnerabilities. In Jesus's time, people feared leprosy, now known as Hansen's disease, above all other illnesses. A sign of the terror it caused is that leprosy is mentioned forty times in the Bible. The causes of leprosy were not known, but it was assumed to have everything to do with having sinned. No one understood that leprosy is not really a skin disease but is, instead, a nerve-tissue disease that can include a problem with sensing pain.[5] Also unknown were the precise ways it could be passed on. As a result, persons with leprosy were shunned, driven out of the city limits, and ignored thereafter.

I see similarities between leprosy and dementia as it is experienced today. We are, of course, subtler in the ways we isolate persons, especially in late-stage dementia. Rather than putting them outside the city walls, people living with dementia are in the back—in the less-visible sections of our long-term care facilities. One local church-related care facility in Virginia, were I currently live, recently tore down its old nursing home in order to place healthier residents in the front, as part of the newer facility by the street. Those with dementia and other serious illnesses were then moved to the rear, out of sight. We have our own ways of ignoring and shunning those who are no longer beautiful by our cultural standards, and who remind us of our intellectual and physical vulnerabilities.

But we also have people who offer a Christ-like presence in nursing homes and in private homes. They are the people like Bonnie, Elenore, Sally, and Sam—caregivers who show up, stroke a cheek, read a Bible verse, and quietly care for physical and emotional needs. Bonnie once told me that when she runs out of patience, she prays. She said:

> One day I thought to myself, I just can't hear that same story again! This woman is just too ornery! So, I went into the bathroom and prayed, "Jesus give me the strength to listen to this woman! She is all alone!" Then I went out and said to her, "Why don't you take a nice bath and then we'll play cards!" That worked just fine.

Is dementia the new leprosy?

Bonnie is not perfect—she gets tired, too. But she has the model of Christ's love, the support of her community, and the assurances that she is herself loved and forgiven to keep her going. And she certainly knows when to pray!

Prayer and Love

Like Bonnie, I am a frequent prayer. Formal communal prayer, regular devotions, and spontaneous chats with God are all life-long practices. But I don't think I have ever prayed so often or so desperately as when I was caring for my mother-in-law, Jessyee. She moved into our home soon after her ninetieth birthday, just weeks after she left the hospital. She had fallen down the stairs in her own home and broken her neck, necessitating a neck brace and daily care as she healed. Jessyee didn't have dementia until many years later, in her nineties (yes, she was a survivor), but I experienced some of the challenges that all caregivers face while she stayed with us, beginning with problems with managing my time. I was on sabbatical that year and was hoping that in the time away from teaching, I could finish writing a book. Then everything changed overnight when Jessyee's need for twenty-four-hour care arose.

Prayer was my primary resource. I found it such a relief to admit my own selfishness and resentment in conversations with God, and to confess and ask for forgiveness each day. I didn't feel completely free to talk to my husband or children about all my feelings, especially those emotions that were unattractive, even to me—resentment (that my time was interrupted), insecurity (that I might not be able to manage her care), and irritability (that she didn't seem to appreciate my great, noble sacrifice—yes, I think I believed that on some childish level). I was partially motivated by my family's hopes and expectations, and somewhat by my own sense of being called to this work, along with good old Lutheran guilt. My motives were mixed, but there was one motivation that saved the day—I truly loved my mother-in-law.

No two people could have been more different than were Jan and Jessyee Ramsey. One was a Yankee who lived primarily in the world of ideas and books; one was a Southern woman whose favorite pastimes were cooking beans and talking with her sisters on the phone. Yet, we connected and loved each other as best we could—at first, because we both loved her son, but eventually because we connected as women, as human beings, as members of our family and of God's. Caregiving brought us together and drew us even closer over time.

As the days passed that year, there were times I had to laugh at my own selfish thoughts and irritability. How could a gerontologist be so impatient working with an old woman? What good did all that theory do if I couldn't put it into practice? But, looking back, I believe I was a good enough caregiver.[6] Jessyee seemed happy with us, so I must have enacted more love than resentment. I guess I eventually got on the train with her, as Elenore would put it. I cooked (lots of protein to heal those bones), helped her bathe and toilet, found simple tasks for her to do (shelling beans), and accompanied her on walks around our neighborhood. But it wasn't easy. I also cried sometimes when I was alone, and I will admit to fantasies of jumping in the car and taking off. We most certainly do not leave our humanity behind when we become full-time caregivers!

> We most certainly do not leave our humanity behind when we become full-time caregivers!

Looking back, it was a privilege to accompany such a brave and feisty woman, and it helped me understand caregiving in ways I could not through academics or professional experiences alone. Most importantly, I am convinced that I couldn't have done it without prayer, prayer that brought me closer to the love and forgiveness of God. This prayer also helped me give thanks for the love for Jessyee that God put into my selfish heart.

Caregiving is a tough, tough business and requires tough, tough love (along with tough hope—please see the afterword). Tender feelings alone don't get us through. Some of the worst impediments come from within us. Only the grace of God is strong enough to get us through as we try to show more love than irritability on each complicated day we give care.

Special Challenges to Gracious Love

I know I was spared many challenges during my caregiving experience because my mother-in-law did not have dementia at that point in her life. Listening to the caregivers who have come to my counseling office over the years and reflecting on the interviews I conducted recently have left me with a deep appreciation for the unique challenges caregivers face when dealing with dementia. It is always important to know what we are up against and that, for caregivers and their care partners, living with grace is every bit as difficult as living with dignity. But we also know that it is vital to solve the challenges to love in the context of dementia care because the experience of having dementia is "as much relational and social as it is neurological."[7] Without the comfort of respectful, loving relationships, the cloud of dementia is far denser.

Why is it so difficult to love those who are living with dementia? Some reasons are similar to difficulties whenever we care with the elderly. It is hard to see the end of the current problem in this work. When caring for the very young, we at least have the knowledge that they will become more and more independent, while with the very old, the future holds only increasing physical decline. At times, their physical needs are urgent and make us weary. We hope they will not ring that bell or call for us one more time. Yet, there are many gifts for those of us who choose to give care—beginning with the realization that we are following Jesus's example.

The caregivers I have met usually sense this need for love. I have witnessed their courage as they worked to enact love. At times with my counsel, but most times alone, they have found creative approaches to the difficulties dementia presents to our efforts to love well. I am delighted to share some of these possibilities with you here. I call them possibilities because they are not formulas or

Only the grace of God is strong enough to get us through as we try to show more love than irritability on each complicated day we give care.

> **Challenges to Loving in the Presence of Dementia**
> - Personality changes
> - Role changes
> - Changes in familiar activities
> - Forgotten stories

universal solutions. Each person living with dementia is unique, and each caregiver differs from all others.

Personality Changes

One of the most confusing and distressing changes occurring with persons experiencing dementia is dramatic alterations in personality. If the frontal lobe is impacted by the disease, personality changes, including decreased impulse control, are likely to be noticeable. These changes also vary because of the type of dementia. For example, Lewy body disease, a lesser-known dementia-causing disease, tends to cause hallucinations that radically impact the personality and behavior. Personality changes also vary by stage of the disease. Persons with early stage Alzheimer's can become suspicious, fearful, or unusually dependent on their caregivers. Rapid shifts in mood are common and create confusion for both the caregiver and her care partner with dementia.[8] Although not all personality changes are negative, positive changes are less remarkable and problematic for family and professional caregivers. It is the changes that are perceived as negative that inspire caregivers to seek a medical evaluation and, at times, to find help from a professional counselor or social worker.

As a nursing-home chaplain, I was surprised to learn that Emma, who had advanced Alzheimer's disease, was a quiet, polite person who would not have dreamed of speaking roughly earlier in her life. I was shocked because I knew Emma as the woman who frequently hurled curses at the staff and anyone else who walked by her room. Another challenge was presented by Mary, a woman with Parkinson's-related dementia, who began to shout racial slurs at the (mostly African American) nursing assistants. (I strongly suspected, and her son confirmed, that the prejudice had always been there but under verbal control.) On another occasion, a woman in my counseling office, Helen, told me tearfully about living with her husband's short temper. He had never been the most patient person in the world, but in the presence of dementia he had become far more irritable and short-tempered.

It is easy to recognize how challenging these personality changes were for their professional and personal caregivers. The behaviors of Mary and Helen's husband are more typical than the story of Emma, because life-long personality traits often become more exaggerated, rather than completely transformed, in early stage dementia. A bossy person becomes more controlling, and a quiet, sweet person becomes even quieter and sweeter.[9] But whether the changes are dramatic or gradual, they make the daily lives of caregivers more arduous.

The stories of Emma, Mary, and Helen are some of the most memorable from my clinical experiences, but I have heard numerous others. What caregivers have in common is the desire to continue to give gracious care to those they love, rather than to overreact to troubling personality changes. This is far from easy, but there are strategies that help.

It is crucial to begin by reminding ourselves that what we are witnessing is the result of changes in the brain, not voluntary changes in a personality. These alterations are beyond the control of the person living with dementia. Education on just how the changes happen and on what other people have done to cope with them is a great way to begin. I have often referred caregivers to the free online materials created by the Alzheimer's Association; these materials apply to all persons with dementia, not only those with Alzheimer's disease (see the resources at the back of this book). Visualizing the brain as wounded and broken can also be helpful.

My favorite tool to teach caregivers, however, is called "externalizing the problems." Since I specialized in chronic illness

> What caregivers have in common is the desire to continue to give gracious care to those they love, rather than to overreact to troubling personality changes.

in my clinical practice as a marriage-and-family therapist, I often worked with families and couples trying to cope with changes resulting from disease, including multiple sclerosis, HIV, and Alzheimer's disease. During those years, I adapted a technique from one of the pioneers in narrative therapy, the Australian Michael White. White noticed that many of the people who sought his help as a family therapist "believe that the problems in their lives are a reflection of their own identity or the identity of others."[10] White believed that simply talking over problems would make things worse. He also saw his clients' symptoms as a battle against the objectification of people in many cultural practices (reminding me of how ageism can exacerbate our problems with love).

On the other hand, externalizing our problems shifts our view of how we relate to our problems. Now the symptom, not the person, becomes the problem. These conversations separate the person (who is distressed) from their symptoms (for example, angry outbursts) by visualizing the problem as "out there," rather than inside the person. Thus, people in distress can move from blaming themselves or others to blaming the problem.

White trained many therapists to use rich and flexible narrative techniques such as externalization. But I found that it is possible to use a simplified version of externalization with caregivers who are feeling stuck with their emotional reactions. (I do not recommend attempting to teach this process to most people diagnosed with dementia, since it requires the ability to sequence.)

I like to use an actual object when teaching people how to externalize a problem—maybe a stone or a piece of paper or something else relevant to the issue. I suggest they place it on the floor, at a distance from themselves. Then I suggest we name the object after a symptom: "That's your anger out there," or, "That's your impatience with this disease." People untangle themselves and their family members quickly from the problem itself in this way, and then we can form a team to understand the impact of the problem and work on ways to cope. I began with a series of

People in distress can move from blaming themselves or others to blaming the problem.

Steps to Externalizing a Problem

1. Place an object close by.

2. Name it for a problem or symptom.

3. Suggest that we form a team to combat the problem.

4. Discuss how the problem is impacting each person's life.

5. Find times when the problem is not in control.

6. Wonder together about how to increase the times when the problem is not in charge.

questions, including "How does anger try to take over your life?" I then move on to what is called searching for exceptions: "Are there times you are able to resist letting that anger take over?" Finally, I wonder with them what might have to change to increase these times of exception.

This technique can help caregivers visualize their situations in new ways and learn to focus their own anger and impatience where it belongs—on the illness itself. A lightbulb moment occurs when someone realizes that she has a choice—not about living with the disease, but in how she reacts to the problematic symptoms the disease presents. Best of all, she can cease thinking of the person she cares for as the problem. A sense of safe space between caregiver and her care partner is created, and partnerships deepen when the enemy is moved to the outside—that is, externalized. This way of coping is easily learned and can be done by caregivers with individual help or in groups of caregivers. It calls for playfulness and creativity that also help break through the sad and overly tragic atmosphere that personality changes often bring.

Role Changes

Dementia takes a toll not only on individual family members but also on the entire family system. When I first met Natalie, dementia was not the immediate concern. It was her marriage. She and her husband, Brad, were both successful professionals but were in acute distress—sitting apart in the office, frowning often, unable to speak to each other without sarcasm and anger. They each had a litany of complaints, and it took several weeks for me to discern that the roots of the problem lay in Natalie's invisible grief. She was raised in a prosperous family in the deep South as the favorite of her father, who not only showered her with material gifts but also gave her obvious affection and took an interest in her life. "Daddy was a real Southern gentleman," she explained, "and he loved me and, I'll admit, spoiled me too." Then Natalie's father developed early onset Alzheimer's disease. "I had to watch him slowly disappear," she said through her tears. When he was moved to a long-term care facility in a distant state, she felt unable to visit him or help her sisters plan his care. Natalie felt paralyzed; she simply could not move from the role of being cared for into the role of caregiver.

Now Natalie's marriage was failing because she expected her husband, Brad, to give her the same attention, affection, and material gifts that she had always had from her father. Merely failing to open the door for Natalie would get Brad into trouble for days. She felt guilty for not being involved in her father's care but little guilt for how she was punishing Brad for her own loss. Not surprisingly, marital work took several years and had to be combined with individual therapy.

When someone is diagnosed with dementia, roles must change and losses must be assimilated. Most stories are less dramatic than that of Natalie; most people find more mature ways to cope with role changes. But I have heard many people confess how much they miss a mother's attention, a spouse's help, a father's admiration. Love changes as roles change, and that is far from easy. Love for an adult caregiver now means being the primary one who gives, cares, and attends to the other. This was something Natalie had to learn to do, at midlife, since she had not learned it as a young adult. Dementia was a plot breaker for her and for her extended family, as it so often is.

> Dementia takes a toll not only on individual family members but also on the entire family system.

How do we best cope with the changes in roles that dementia brings? This is one challenge for which there is no simply strategy. We can certainly begin by trying to figure out, as Natalie did, just why we are so distressed. To cope with a change from being cared for by a parent to caring for a parent is especially difficult because it involves the ongoing process we call *growing up*.

Life happens while we are making other plans, and when a young person in pain goes for pastoral counseling, she is not likely to talk about the chance that she will someday have a parent with dementia—let alone work on issues of personal maturity. Showing love as a grown-up has little to do with chronological age and everything to do with learning to both care for yourself and to empathize with the needs of others.

There are possibilities for speeding up the process of developing empathy for others. One is to assume more responsibility at an early age. Children who must care for younger siblings have to grow up quickly, at times too quickly. I am convinced that a liberal-arts education, travel abroad, and reading widely, especially classical literature, are also paths to maturity. But how do we know if we have grown up? There is no universal marker in our culture that proves we're grown ups, ready for role changes. Not even marriage, a first job, or becoming a parent guarantees that we are mature.

Ironically, caregiving for someone with dementia pushes us to move into adulthood. The experience of living with and accepting role changes can provide a dramatic shove toward maturity. But role changes require patience, acceptance, and empathy. Often, they require outside family counseling because they call forth deep, primordial hurts that are beyond our everyday awareness, as they were for Natalie. I think role changes may be among the most difficult adjustments required by family members caring for those with dementia.

> When someone is diagnosed with dementia, roles must change and losses must be assimilated.

Changes in Familiar Activities

Perhaps you and your father had a custom to have dinner together at least once a month, but now he has dementia and becomes agitated and distressed in restaurants. Or maybe you and your partner liked to play cards with friends, but recently she can't remember what suit is trump and she leaves the group in a huff. Dementia forces caregivers and their family member with dementia to find new ways to be together, and that isn't easy.

My mother and I lived in different states for most of my adult life; fortunately, my brother and sister lived close to her. We had developed a family ritual that we all loved. When I came to visit, everyone would gather to eat an amazing chocolate cake, baked with love by my mother. (It is still called Mimi's Chocolate Cake in our extended family.) Then my mother developed vascular dementia. She continued to cook, but the last time she tried to make the chocolate cake, it looked more like a piece of cardboard than a cake. Mimi didn't seem to be troubled by the failed cake, but she never made another one. Eating homemade cake together was such a little thing, yet so symbolic of the losses we were facing as a family as her dementia progressed.

Each family where dementia is present has stories like the one of Mimi and the chocolate cake—about activities that were precious and seem even more precious after they are no longer possible. We grieve their loss, but we also come to accept them and move on. We find ways to do things together that do *not* rely on short-term memory—do not require sequenced actions. For example, after that failed cake day, my mother and I would go to a bakery and buy a cake to share with the family (comparing it unfavorably with her own, of course).

There are substitute activities that do not lead to frustration and failure for persons with dementia and their families, or for their professional caregivers (see the resources at the back of the book). Watching a favorite TV show together is an old reliable activity

Role changes require patience, acceptance, and empathy.

and one that requires little input; sports broadcasts work especially well. Walking around a familiar neighborhood or along a park path, visiting an art gallery, sorting simple items around the home, or experiencing music together—these are possible rich and stimulating activities. The important thing is to not give up when one activity falls as flat as our cake but to keep trying to simplify until you are again doing something enjoyable together. When the activity is chosen based on the interests of the person with an impaired memory, all the better.

Forgotten Stories

When you are caring for someone who has shared many years of life with you, it is painful to realize that this person's impaired memory now makes it difficult for them to remember the times of your lives. As we get older, we like to remember the important and not-so-important events that bind us together, give us joy, and remind us of where we came from. Even in families where there has been a tragedy, these memories are important, as we know from hearing of flood and fire victims who carried with them their most important treasures—the family photos.

But how do we do this remembering without the mother, the father, the partner, with whom we have shared so many moments? The fact that they are still physically present but can't remember can make this loss even more poignant. In casual conversations, we want to say, "Remember when Carry lost the dog and then we found him curled up on the sofa at home?" but then realize that no, she cannot remember that night. In fact, she may not even remember the name of her daughter, Carry. Small wonder that the social world of persons with dementia so often shrinks radically, as easy reminiscence fades.

Another danger, especially for professional caregivers, can arise in trying to encourage a person living with dementia to reminisce. You may stumble onto a memory that is painful or even traumatic for them. As a nursing-home chaplain, I learned this the hard way. I was fond of a woman with early stage dementia and agreed to take her to visit her home church in the country. I was excited, thinking it would be a great day for her. But when we walked into the little cemetery beside the church, she burst into tears. "I didn't know he had passed!" she told me when looking at the grave marker of a relative who had been dead for many years. I was forcing her to grieve all over again.

Both persons with memory loss and their caregivers must grieve. Each new day brings another change, another loss. Loving someone with dementia means having to grieve often, but it also means going on, trying to find alternative ways to be doing something together, using as much knowledge and flexibility as we can manage. Fortunately, there are resources for most of our challenges, even for those with mid- to late-stage dementia. A recent conversation with my daughter, Dr. Katherine Luci, a geropsychologist, taught me that geropsychologists, activity directors, occupational therapists, and others have developed and are developing exciting ways to do life review with persons with dementia. Life-story books and activities that do not depend on chronological events can be used even after dementia has fractured the chronological connections between life events.

Using photo albums or old magazines at home is an easy and reliable way to make emotional connections between the person with dementia and their caregiver. It is not necessary to be able to tie the memories together neatly, and sometimes the caregiver will be remembering events that are very different from those in the mind of the person with cognitive issues. That's ok! Living in a family and talking with my five adult children has taught me that everyone's memory is different, even without dementia. The important thing is the emotional connection—the love that binds us together—not the factual details.

Focusing on music, the smells of a favorite dish cooking, a painting on a wall—there are so many ways to help persons with dementia enjoy the moment. Be creative and take your time. Activities are possible and enjoyable for those who will risk entering the world of someone with imperfect memories.

Loving someone with dementia means having to grieve often, but it also means going on, trying to find alternative ways to be doing something together, using as much knowledge and flexibility as we can manage.

Love and Couples

Anyone who thinks that romantic love disappears when dementia appears has not spent much time in a long-term care facility. On the other hand, anyone who thinks romantic love is all there is in marriage is doomed for disappointment, with or without the presence of dementia. I proceed with caution here as I begin to explore romantic love, simply because it is such a complicated subject.

Dementia presents profound trials for couples. All the changes described above—in personality, roles, life stories, and activities—are everyday challenges to a couple that has been together for many years. Living with the changes that dementia brings, couples must find new ways to behave and even to feel. The confusion about how to relate to each other now cannot be fully understood by anyone who has not experienced caregiving and dementia. What it means to be a loving couple must be redefined, and couples must learn to cherish moments of shared joy in the present over those they shared in the past.

Even a couple's friendship networks are impacted. Some groups of friends are more tolerant and sophisticated about aging-related changes in general and dementia in particular. These friends continue to exercise hospitality to those couples experiencing dementia. Others begin to exclude them. Similar to what divorcing persons often experience, couples with a member who has dementia may find themselves noting that there is no longer room at the table for them. The invitations for dinner and parties stop, and activities become limited to the couple only.

Most poignant is the arrival of the day when a partner can no longer recall your name or seem to recognize who you are. What a chasm there is between this day and the day you married! Here again we need a new word for the love between couples living with dementia, since it means something quite different after dementia shows up.

> What it means to be a loving couple must be redefined, and couples must learn to cherish moments of shared joy in the present over those they shared in the past.

The caregiving member of the couple often needs outside support in the light of all these changes. A close, lifelong friend may understand better than anyone what you are experiencing and love you enough to listen for many hours. Or you may begin to attend a support group, such as those available at the Alzheimer's Association, or seek out caregivers in similar situations. Either way, it is crucial to get support and remain engaged with other persons rather than relying only on your spouse. It is not fair to either of you to expect them to meet all your needs. This is true of all marriages, but especially so when dementia is present.

Sexuality and Dementia

Sexuality raises issues that are complicated by dementia. Even in the course of normal aging, there are changes in the type and level of intimacy between couples. But when dementia is present, there is a constant need to adjust. What gave a couple closeness, health, and happiness in the past may no longer fit both their current needs.

Personality change that results from alterations in the frontal lobe (less impulse control) is the challenge that seems to be most difficult for some couples. When the person with dementia becomes overly aggressive—or, on the other hand, completely disinterested in sexual intimacy—it is important for the caregiver not to personalize or feel guilty if the partner no longer wishes to have sexual intimacy. On the other hand, sexual relations should not be forced by a caregiver onto the person with dementia, who may well be too confused or physically compromised to participate freely and safely. Some couples find that replacing sexual intercourse with intimate, nonsexual cuddling or massage is a way to continue closeness. Taking care of yourself and your partner, and recognizing that there is no one solution for all couples, is a first priority.

Here again the Alzheimer's Association is one of the best places to go for help with sexual intimacy and dementia. Their philosophy is my own: "There can be many beautiful moments with those we love with the disease, but what constitutes those moments

> What gave a couple closeness, health, and happiness in the past may no longer fit both their current needs.

changes."[11] It may be difficult for caregivers to ask for help with this very personal issue, but physicians, geropsychologists, and counselors trained in gerontology are quite comfortable with the topic. They can listen to your concerns and give individual guidance to you and your partner.

Couples' Ethical Issues in Light of Dementia

Romantic love after dementia is part of a couple's life can become very complicated, and it also presents society and the church with new ethical issues. We know, for example, that romantic love is still possible for persons living in long-term care facilities with middle-stage dementia. An article in the *New York Times* got attention with the title, "Seized by Alzheimer's, Then Love."[12] The reporter used the case study of the husband of retired Supreme Court Justice Sandra Day O'Connor, John Jay O'Connor III, who found companionship with a woman in the nursing home where he lived and who often held her hand, even in the presence of his wife. The article raised the question of how family members and especially spouses react to such a development. In the case of Day O'Connor's husband, his son responded on behalf of the family, saying they were happy that Mr. O'Connor seemed to have found rays of contentment in the darkness of his disease. Surely, we need a new understanding of love for a family like the O'Connors.

Romantic love that is felt by long-term caregivers is another topic that is under consideration today. How does a family respond when one parent, living in a nursing home, has been unable to respond for many years, and the other parent, the caregiver, has fallen in love with someone else? Should we now say, "Till Dementia Do Us Part," asks a reporter for AARP?[13] What solutions might make sense socially and religiously in such a situation? I hope Christian ethicists will tackle this question and others related to marriage and dementia soon.

Love for Pets and Those Who Have Died

If I were to enter a long-term care facility as a person with dementia tomorrow, I know that one of the most upsetting aspects of the move would be the loss of my pet. Life without my neurotic, loveable, three-legged sheltie would be bereft of much humor and delight. Only recently have facilities begun to be more flexible in allowing residents to keep pets, or at least have "pet days" when animals are brought into the facilities. But this is love, too—and for many persons with dementia, loss of a pet is a tragic and unnecessary loss. What better way to show love to a person with dementia than to permit contact with beloved pets?

Another love that is not often realized is the love that remains for friends and family now deceased. The lines between who is living and who is dead are often blurred for those with memory impairment. The impulse of caregivers is to pull back, or change the topic, when persons with dementia want to talk about parents, spouses, or friends we know to be dead for many years. What better way to show love to a person with dementia than to join in a conversation about a deceased love one?

The Gift of Loving Others

We often speak of how wonderful it is to be loved, but less obvious are the ways that we ourselves benefit when we give love to others. Although it is important to be realistic when we consider the complexities of being a loving caregiver in the face of dementia, we also need to celebrate the benefits.

The feeling of loving someone outside of ourselves is itself a wonderful dimension to our emotional lives. Not only the first rush of emotion in romantic love, not only the close bonds of love between parent and child, but the love we feel for dear friends and extended family are blessings that no one can take from us. This beautiful feeling of giving love is a real joy.

Too often we think of love in solely individual terms, as between only two people. But the emotional and enacted love of caregiving is a benefit to the whole world. When I give a public presentation on caregiving, I always begin by thanking the caregivers in the audience. This typically causes tears, because it shocks people to be thanked. But I am speaking from the heart, because where would we be, as communities and nations, without those who give love to the most vulnerable among us? I thank God for all of you caregivers reading this book, and I pray you will receive the strength and wisdom you need to keep on loving.

Reflection on Psalm 107:1–9, 43

O give thanks to the Lord, for he is good;
for his loving kindness endures forever.
Let the redeemed of the Lord say so,
those he redeemed from trouble
And gathered in from the lands,
from the east and from the west,
from the north and from the south
Some wandered in desert wastes,
finding no way to an inhabited town;
Hungry and thirsty,
their soul fainted within them.
Then they cried to the Lord in their trouble,
and he delivered them from their distress;
He led them by a straight way,
until they reached an inhabited town
Let them thank the Lord for his steadfast love,
for his wonderful works to humankind.
For he satisfies the thirsty,
and the hungry he fills with good things.
. . . .
Let those who are wise give heed to these things,
And consider the steadfast love [*hesed*] of the Lord.

THIS PSALM is, of course, a literal song, meant to be sung by a
congregation. I like to imagine that the first vocalists who sang
these words were people who knew God, but also folks who knew
that their own attempts to love were far from perfect. They were

wanderers, both literally and figuratively. They had been through some frightening experiences and were now thinking back to their deliverance by God, as they came together and formed a spiritual community. They were so grateful, they simply had to sing.

I picture a stage for this song and place the actors on it. Despite all they had been through, the singers focus not on themselves but on the God who loved them and has accomplished wonderful works on their behalf. They recognize that God not only brought them to safety but loved them so much that he satisfied their hunger and thirst. We are wise indeed, as the psalm proclaims, to pay attention to the steadfast love of the Lord. In my imaginative play, God is clearly on center stage.

When I become discouraged by the horrors of the evening news, when I see my friends suffering from the cruelty of persons they trusted, or when I am dismayed by the pain that an illness like dementia causes, I need Psalm 107. I need to be reminded of God's steadfast love. I need to give heed to what God has done, to place God on center stage in my life and in my worship and refocus on what is trustworthy—namely, God's steadfast love.

This psalm tells of wandering and coming home. I think here first of Mr. H, who told me that he felt like a wanderer (see chapter 1). Dementia does that to people; it confuses them and sets them adrift. But there is no sharp divide between those with dementia and the rest of us when it comes to wandering. Who of us has not wandered at some time? Who of us has can deny that she has repeatedly gone astray, gotten off track, and been in some sort of trouble? But whether this wandering is true literally, as for the Jews in the desert, or figuratively, as for the rest of us, the same God leads us all home. And when we arrive, God prepares a feast for us, just to celebrate our arrival. This is the feast of victory for our Lord.

Luther said we need a life of continual repentance if we are to be good lovers of the Lord, and I agree. We love only imperfectly and with many disruptions. We place ourselves and our little issues center stage. We need someone in our community to yank us off the center of our own stage—just as bad actors were pulled off the Vaudeville stage with a long hook. We are not the source of all things; we are not the heroes in our own story. Divine love must be at the center if we don't want to write a tragic plot for our little life play. We may love, but not with the steadfast love—the *hesed*—that is God's own.

The word *hesed*, steadfast love, occurs thirty-two times in the psalter, which tells us something about its importance. *Hesed* does not have one single meaning but implies that we are in desperate need of help from someone who is utterly dependable.[1] That's the difference between our love, even at its best, and the love of God. We love as we can and when we will. God can't help loving all the time, because that's who God is.

There are people in our lives who give us glimpses of the steadfast love we know in perfect form from God. Sometimes we see this love in parents, grandparents, a spouse, or a special teacher or friend. I like to think that many of us have had pastors, or other congregational leaders, who have modeled devotion and selfless love, but not all of us are that lucky. I am among the fortunate ones, because I did.

His name was Gil Jensen, and he was my pastor in Fairfield, California, where I had just moved when I was about twenty-eight years old. I met him at a low point in my life, a few months after my first pregnancy ended with a premature birth. We lost our baby girl soon after she was born, because the technology to save low-weight premature babies had not yet been developed. Although I had been raised in a parsonage, I was no longer attending church regularly, but my grief led me into a Lutheran church service. It turned out to be a place where love was found.

Most of the members of St. Mark's in Fairfield had been through some sort of difficulty in their lives. They had wandered off before coming to this congregation. Gil, who was also a pastoral counselor, had the skills, energy, and compassion to create a loving community—one I have never seen so clearly before or since.

We love as we can and when we will. God can't help loving all the time, because that's who God is.

He was deeply anchored in his Christian faith and worked long hours when he was needed by those in distress. This pastor taught me, along with all the members of that church, to find ways to be honest with each other, but more importantly, to place God at the center of our lives. Gradually, our problems seemed less tragic and the future more promising. It was the steadfast love of God, embodied in this pastor, that led me to decide to go to seminary and become a pastoral counselor. Best of all, at St. Mark's, I felt that I had come home for the first time in my life.

Perhaps you already have a community that is your home. I don't mean a home that is literally where you live, but a spiritual home— one that you can go to in your heart, even years later, and heed again to God's steadfast love. Keep wandering if you have not yet located such a community, because it is priceless. And don't be fooled by leaders who place themselves on center stage. That's where God and God alone belongs. You'll know when you find it, because you'll hear words like this: "He led them by a straight way, until they reached an inhabited town. Let them thank the Lord for his steadfast love, for his wonderful works to humankind. For he satisfies the thirsty, and the hungry he fills with good things."

5

If Only . . . : Grace and Forgiveness

IF LOVE is what we need and want, not only as caregivers but as human beings, what happens when love fails? What happens when we are hurt by the very person we trusted and relied on? Can there be grace in our lives when love has *not* provided security and peace in a relationship? Is resilient caregiving possible when a caregiver feels like a victim—not only because of her current role, but especially because she is still suffering from unresolved past hurts?

Alice and Harry, a couple I counseled in the Midwest, are struggling with a past that is complicating their present. Harry has dementia related to his many years of alcohol abuse, and as Alice cares for him in their home, she often feels victimized and resentful. Although she meets his physical needs, their emotional life together is fractured by the plot of their old story: his drinking, her failed attempts to "make him stop," and now the presence of the very physical and mental problems she anticipated for years.

Alice told me that she feels guilty "because sometimes I'm so irritable with him." She also reports that Harry says, "I'm so sorry," over and over, throughout the day—but for no apparent reason. With a limited memory of the past and decreasing verbal skills now, Harry is not able to have genuine conversations with her about their marriage. And their roles have changed. For the first time, she must now make the important choices in their lives, such as the recent decision to sell their summer house at the lake. Alice is not sure she wants all this responsibility; she has mixed feelings about being in charge. Above all, she wishes she and Harry had a different past.

Alice and Harry's adult children know about Harry's years of alcohol abuse but wish that Alice could put her feelings aside. "They don't get it. They think it's simply a matter of overlooking years of unhappiness," Alice says. She shows a wide range of emotions— guilt (at her anger, which she sees as proof that she has not forgiven Harry), relief (that the drinking days are finally past), and longing (that someday her caregiving responsibilities will finally end).

Alice is a Christian, active in her congregation, and devoted to living out her faith. She told me she knows she is getting the help she needs from God with the physical demands of caregiving, and emotional support from her friends at church—none of whom know about the alcoholism. Still, she feels she isn't living out the central teaching of her faith: forgiveness.

During our counseling sessions, I couldn't help thinking, "If only . . ." If only this couple had joined AA and Al-Anon. If only they had sought marital counseling earlier, from someone who worked with substance-abuse issues. If only they had been able to work through this thorny forgiveness issue before Harry became cognitively impaired. But the past cannot be changed and, as Alice says, "Here I am." She feels stuck, imprisoned by her own resentment.

It is easy to empathize with Alice and her years of struggle, as well as her current feelings. It is also possible to empathize with Harry, who is now disempowered and unable to make amends for the hurts he caused. Is there any way for this couple to begin living with God's grace in their last years together? Is there any way for Alice to forgive Harry, even when he can no longer fully participate in a reconciliation process? Does the ability to forgive require repentance by the one who injured us? And how can a person like Alice stop feeling like a victim?

> If love is what we need and want, not only as caregivers but as human beings, what happens when love fails?

Each relationship—for both the person living with dementia and her caregiver—has a unique history that then becomes part of the caregiving dynamics. Not only married couples, but children and parents or other family members and close friends—all go into the experience of dementia care with a story that is complicated. Even when there is little awareness of resentment, unresolved old hurts can surface at times that surprise caregivers and threaten to detract from the grace of intimate relationships. We may wish, at times, that we could tear out a few pages from the mental scrapbook of our lives. Of course, we cannot change the past. There is only one way to break free of its negative pull on us: forgiveness.

A Christian Treasure

The rabbi faced his audience, paused, and then said quietly, "I wonder if you Christians know what a treasure you have. I confess that I am a bit envious of your belief in a God so filled with mercy that he can forgive even the most horrible sinner. This is a real treasure of your theology."[1]

These words continue to echo in my mind after I heard them in 2004 at an Extended Conference on Forgiveness at Tantur Ecumenical Institute in Jerusalem. Rabbi Levi Weiman-Kelman is an American Reformed rabbi who now serves a Reformed congregation in Israel. He began to dialogue, many years ago, with a few Muslim and Christian clergy, risking both his reputation and physical safety to work for peace and forgiveness in Jerusalem, a city of extreme brokenness. I immediately respected this rabbi for his courage, but also for his haunting perspective on Christianity, a point of view even more remarkable considering the long, troubled history of Jewish-Christian relations. Speaking that day to a primarily Christian audience of scholars, he raised for us two crucial realities—the "treasure" of forgiveness in Christianity, and his wondering if we recognize that treasure.

There is no doubt that forgiveness is central to Christian theology, both as it has been described by centuries of biblical scholars and as

Each relationship—for both the person living with dementia and her caregiver—has a unique history that then becomes part of the caregiving dynamics.

it is preached and taught today. Like all the world's major religions, Christianity calls for forgiveness, but there are significant differences among Christians, Jews, and Muslims.[2] Jews, for example, must forgive only if the offender repents and asks for forgiveness. Muslims are required to forgive with the exception of people who are working against Islam or denying Muslim principles.[3]

The wrongdoer's repentance is not a requirement in Christianity, while the command to forgive is unconditional and radical. Scripture teaches, over and over, that forgiveness was won by Jesus, at great cost and with enormous implications. Jesus is remembered as the one who forgave his enemies even while he was being executed in a horrible fashion. He was the one whose mission was to usher in a new day of forgiveness and love. In the Lord's Prayer, the prayer that is prayed daily by Christians around the world, the need for forgiveness is ranked as equally important to physical needs. Yes, Christians have this treasure.

However, the degree to which we Christians appreciate our forgiveness theology is less obvious. The complex history of Christianity reveals a complicated, unattractive answer: *sometimes yes, sometimes no*. Sometimes Christians have proclaimed forgiveness to a broken world with both words and deeds. One thinks, for example, of Bishop Tutu's truth and reconciliation work after the end of apartheid in South Africa. But other times, although the church continued to preach forgiveness, Christian love for this theological treasure has been anything but clear. Returning to Africa for an opposite example, we witnessed the horrific behavior of church leaders in Rwanda, long part of the system of colonialism, who either condoned or even participated in the Hutu genocide against the Tutsi.[4] Our forgiveness history is uneven and sometimes tragic.

At the personal level, too, the answer is complex. When we, as individual Christians, not only forgive those who hurt us at particular moments of a relationship crisis but also cherish forgiveness as a lifelong practice, we are the joyful people who value our treasure. The entire nation was moved by the reaction of

The wrongdoer's repentance is not a requirement in Christianity, while the command to forgive is unconditional and radical.

the Amish community in Lancaster, Pennsylvania, after a gunman senselessly shot ten girls in a one-room schoolhouse. "The afternoon of the shooting an Amish grandfather of one of the girls who was killed expressed forgiveness toward the killer, Charles Roberts. That same day Amish neighbors visited the Roberts family to comfort them in their sorrow and pain."[5] Similarly, after the shooting of nine innocent victims in an AME church in Charleston, South Carolina, relatives spoke directly to Dylann Roof, who had killed their loved ones. *The Washington Post* reported on Roof's bond hearing:

> "I forgive you," Nadine Collier, the daughter of 70-year-old Ethel Lance, said at the hearing, her voice breaking with emotion. "You took something very precious from me. I will never talk to her again. I will never, ever hold her again. But I forgive you."[6]

When, on the other hand, we are motivated by and caught up in the values of a calculating, revenge-focused world, we become part of the problem of unforgiveness. At such times, we have buried our treasure and returned hurt for hurt, violent word for violent word. Counseling offices, civil courts, and television dramas are filled with examples of unforgiveness too numerous to name. Christians are not excluded from these sad relational dramas. Often the topic of forgiveness is ignored, trivialized, or misused by perpetrators to escape the just consequences of their acts. Perhaps one of the most unattractive, disingenuous sights common today is that of a politician standing at a press conference after his sexual misconduct has been made known to the public, asking for forgiveness with an obviously distressed and hurting—but silent—wife by his side. Is that forgiveness? Is that a model for the work that Alice needs to do?

What Is Forgiveness Anyway?

Forgiveness has been defined in many ways. Most often it is linked to giving up the desire for revenge.[7] Teaching and writing about forgiveness with my colleague Dr. Lois Malcom,[8] I have developed a somewhat different definition, one that reflects both my conviction that forgiving includes suffering, and my belief that often women who wish to forgive (including myself, Alice, and many other women) need to get out of a position of helpless victimhood: Forgiveness is moving from the passive suffering of a victim to the active, hopeful suffering of a survivor who is moving on. Forgiveness is taking the first steps out of a quagmire, not so that we will avoid all pain, but so that God will, in God's own time, transform our pain—both for our own sake and for the sake of others.

Our families, cultures, and histories present to us many pictures of what the world is like. Most of these pictures are based on power, violence, and the need for revenge. But a truer picture of the world includes forgiveness. When we forgive, we don't have to overlook the suffering it entails, because the pain is a crucial piece of the picture of the way things are. But we're searching for a different way to be in the world, a way that is embodied, emotional, and relational. Another name for this way to live is love. When humans forgive, we are echoing Christ's self-emptying love, because when Christ died, forgiveness and love were both enacted. Thus, forgiveness takes us back to where we began, to the capacity for gracious love.

That sounds neat and easy, but nothing could be further from the truth. As I learned over and over in my counseling office, forgiveness is a process, and it is every bit as messy and uneven as love. In some cases, the process of forgiveness cannot be completed in one lifetime (see the story of Michel, below). But Christian life has a pattern. We love a little, we are forgiven much, and we manage to forgive a little. Then we love a little better and a little more—but we again fail to avoid hurting others, and need forgiveness again. Hopefully, somewhere along the story line, we meet Christ, and we respond to the perfect love we see by repenting and following him. But we never forget or leave behind the complications of learning to love and to forgive. That's what makes life so precious—our recognition of how rare are the gifts of self-emptying love and genuine forgiveness.

Forgiveness is moving from the passive suffering of a victim to the active, hopeful suffering of a survivor who is moving on.

> Then Peter came and said to him [Jesus], "Lord, if another member of the church sins against me, how often should I forgive? As many as seven times?" Jesus said to him, "Not seven times, but, I tell you, seventy-seven times."
>
> —Matthew 18:21–22

The Most Difficult Work We Ever Do

As Jesus's response to Peter shows, our need to forgive is far greater than humans expect (seventy-seven symbolizing a large number). Should Alice then say to herself, "I must forgive Harry. I'm certainly not up to seventy-seven yet!" If only forgiving were so easy.

Alice's feelings were deep and long lasting, but not all forgiveness is so difficult because not all hurts are so deep. Sometimes we simply choose to overlook a slight or a careless word, forgiving casually and quickly, hardly noticing what we are doing. Life is simply too short to feel pain over everything. Sometimes in our lives together, especially in the life between a caregiver and a person with dementia, the only way to live graciously is to ignore a great deal of behavior and move on.

The need to overlook small injuries, such as an insensitive word spoken thoughtlessly, is present for both a person living with cognitive problems and for her caregiver. If your caregiver lacks the perfect sensitivity of Amy (see the intro to part 2) or the remarkable patience of Bonnie (see chapter 3), you may feel frustrated and misunderstood. Yet, you know that your care partner can't possibly understand what you are going through, the confusion and irritation that come with impaired memory. So, you ignore your disappointment.

Or, if you are a family or professional caregiver, you may wish that just a few of your many acts of kindness and service would be appreciated and remembered for more than a few moments. Yet, you know it is inevitable that the person with dementia who benefits from those acts of kindness will quickly forget them. You decide to ignore your disappointment. Moving past the smaller hurts that are inevitable in a caregiving situation is simply part of two grown-ups trying to get along. This is something we learn in other close relationships long before we reach old age—as parent and child, as friends, as partners. Not every hurt is a big deal.

On the other hand, we sometimes carry around pain that was caused by serious harm from our past relationships. An affair that took place more than thirty years ago; insulting words spoken by an in-law; financial matters that were not dealt with openly and honestly—these can lead to relational injuries that linger and require active forgiveness. We know we would be happier and more at peace if we could forgive over and over, as Jesus commanded Peter (Matt 18:21–22). But we struggle mightily. Why? What makes forgiveness the most difficult interpersonal work we ever do?

We sometimes hesitate to forgive because we are afraid of being hurt again, thinking that forgiveness is the same as becoming a passive victim of harm. Or we don't want to forgive because we will have to amend our opinions of the one who hurt us. I could see Alice struggling with this one, and she was moving toward balance. She told me about Harry's spiritual life, about how he prays often and always thanks God for her and her care. I glimpsed parts of him that she continues to appreciate, even as she wondered whether she had really forgiven him.

Forgiveness is sometimes costly because we must give up our role as the totally innocent one and wonder if we have any faults of our own. It's hard to give up being a victim, but it's harder still to admit to being a sinner. It is not easy to go to the foot of the cross and say to the other sinners, "Move over—I'm here too." Yet in the end, that is exactly where we are all standing.

Forgiving also requires that we do some editing of our personal narratives. I have always found it fascinating that the stories of victims and of perpetrators are so different, especially regarding the depth of the harm. Victims tend to see the damage done and the pain suffered as far greater than do the perpetrators. But both the person struggling to forgive and the one who committed the harm must redo their stories somewhat to reflect a more ambiguous and complicated event—and all human events are certainly more than meets the eye.

> Moving past the smaller hurts that are inevitable in a caregiving situation is simply part of two grown-ups trying to get along.

> Forgiveness is sometimes costly because we must give up our role as the totally innocent one and wonder if we have any faults of our own.

Of all the reasons that it is tough to forgive, none is more prominent that the desire to avoid the emotional pain (suffering) we feel as we grieve our losses—including the loss of trust in the one who hurt us, the loss of our worldview (in cases of extreme hurt), the loss of our romantic view of the past. Wouldn't it be great if we could forgive without that difficult first step! This difficulty deserves some focus of its own.

Acknowledging that something has been lost can be a difficult first step in the grief process. Most of us don't stop to grieve before we start trying to forgive, only to be later reminded of the depth of our remaining sorrow. We may have thought, or pretended, that we have moved past feelings of victimhood, anger, and hurt, yet suddenly something happens to remind us of what is gone or changed forever, and we feel that we're back at step one, in denial and feeling stuck. Of past hurts reappear in our dreams, suggesting we are not quite finished with them.

For Alice, each day brings reminders of these feelings, even as she tries to care for the very person she sees as the cause of her problems. After years of hurt, and now with the increased time spent together, she no longer can ignore the realities of what is broken, what is gone, and how she feels about her relationship with Harry. It is also likely that she feels isolated, since she must cope with such powerful feelings while the rest of the world, including the person who hurt her, has moved on. In Alice's situation, Harry has moved on to confusion and forgetfulness beyond his control—but moved on, nevertheless. Yet, Alice is stuck with her resentment. Can her faith help? Can Christian faith help any of us who are stuck in the past?

Faith and Forgiveness

Ironic as it sounds, for some people, misunderstandings of Christianity are part of what makes forgiveness so difficult. If we have been taught that Christians must be constantly happy creatures whose lives are all sunshine and calm, if we have been given subtle

> Acknowledging that something has been lost can be a difficult first step in the grief process.

and not-so-subtle messages that being a strong person of faith means that we ought never feel discouraged, then we might attempt to suppress our initial grief and sorrow, worried that it is a sign of weak faith.

Sometimes this message—"Be strong!"—comes to us indirectly, when people who appear to have no apparent difficulties after a loss are presented to us as role models. "Look at Sue. She was married to a disabled husband, and she cared for him for years without complaining!" At other times, people who have not faced a loss may (unconsciously) minimize its impact as a way of self-protection—"That's sad, but we all have a cross to bear"—and we buy into their thinking. I suspect that people who deny the pain of grief and encourage us to get over it are in denial themselves, hoping to convince themselves that they would not suffer too much should they face a similar loss. And how we hate to suffer. From talk shows to pop psychology to simplistic self-help books, the cultural message is to avoid emotional suffering at any cost.

God does not only feel our pain; God carries and transforms it.

On the other hand, Christianity is a powerful resource for finding the courage to face all sorts of truths in our lives, including the reality of suffering. If we understand Jesus, the suffering Messiah who is at the heart of the gospel, if we acknowledge that we forgive only with and through the power of the suffering (and risen) God, emotional pain will neither surprise nor overwhelm us. This is a strange, countercultural understanding we Christians have. We believe that suffering on behalf of others, suffering as the cost of love, can be redemptive.

Our gospel story teaches us that we are not alone, as we sometimes feel when we are in pain. Knowing our painful stories, God grieves with us, feeling the pain of both our own sins, and the wrongs that are done to us. God is with both Harry, in his confusion, and Alice, in her pain. But God does not only feel our pain; God carries and transforms it.

In the previous chapter, we learned how to externalize issues that were trying to take over our lives. But no one can completely shake free of life's difficulties, especially those deep injuries caused by ourselves or others. We may try to place them away from ourselves, but, unlike the caregivers' problems I symbolically placed in the middle of the room, they are too heavy for us to carry alone. Fortunately, we have this assurance: the cross is the ultimate externalization of human problems.

On the cross, God in Christ gathers up all the ways we hurt each other and heals our wounds, precisely through his passion and death. At the same time, "while we were yet sinners" (Rom 5:8), God restores our dignity. Through Christ's work on the cross, we are not only forgiven but also identified with the righteousness of God. This is what theologian Martin Luther called the "fortunate exchange."[9] To greatly simplify Luther's thought, the fortunate exchange is the exchange of human sin for God-given righteousness. "For our sake he made him to be sin who knew no sin, so that in him we might become the righteousness of God" (2 Cor 5:21).

The great story of Good Friday, the story of Christ's broken body that we proclaim each Eucharist (1 Cor 11:24), transforms our individual narratives and our damaged lives. Christ's work makes it possible for us to love one another in our brokenness, rather than childishly splitting those we know into one-sided characters who are all good or all bad. Moving toward this assurance, we can begin to forgive—not by constantly lamenting our victim status but by taking an active and responsible role in crafting our own lives. Sometimes this dependence on Christ's work is particularly needful because the hurt is deep and persistent. I learned this from a client in my counseling practice, whom I will call Michel.

Forgiveness and Re-Storied Lives

When I met Michel, I was immediately impressed with her resiliency. She came to see me in my pastoral counseling office for help with decision making related to caregiving. Earlier, she had cared for her mother, who had cancer, moving temporarily into her parent's home. She described those thirteen months as "difficult

The cross is the ultimate externalization of human problems.

but rewarding." Now, her father had Alzheimer's disease, and there was no one to care for him at home because her siblings both had health concerns. At first, Michel described this as a situation that was clearly one she could manage—but then I heard of the great sorrow in her life.

Michel grew up in a close family that seemed, to her and to her community, healthy and whole. Then, at the age of forty, she discovered a dreadful secret: her father had, for many years, sexually abused several young family members, including one of her own children. She was horrified by this revelation and found the days that followed this discovery difficult to endure. (At one point she was hospitalized with symptoms of an apparent heart attack, but found that the pains were caused by anger and anxiety.) Trust in the father she knew and loved was shattered. She grieved, feeling robbed of her family memories, her present peace of mind, and her dreams of any happy father-daughter relationship in the future.

For many years, Michel struggled with emotional and spiritual pain, exacerbated by her inability to speak openly of what had happened in order protect the abuse victims, who did not want to be exposed. She often thought that forgiving after we learn that someone we love has been hurt is far more difficult than when we ourselves are the victims. Only gradually was she able to move into a more healthy and whole life, realizing slowly that she had to grieve the past she could not change and let go of her anger or she would become ill herself.

Today, at seventy, Michel is calm and happy and would be physically able to withstand the demands of caregiving. She has a happy marriage and a meaningful vocation, and she has been nurtured by the love of children and friends. Central to her strength is her spiritual life. During the weeks she came to my pastoral counseling office, I heard a variety of ways in which the stories, symbols, and practices of faith have facilitated her move past anger and hurt. I heard wisdom in her narratives that has helped me in my own aging process and with my own efforts to forgive.

> Forgiving after we learn that someone we love has been hurt is far more difficult than when we ourselves are the victims.

Michel eventually decided to support her father's care financially, but not to become his personal caregiver. She had to work to separate her own idea of what was the right thing to do from what she knew others would think—especially those in the family who had no knowledge of the sexual abuse. She was content and at peace with her decision and taught me that caregiving decisions need to be as varied as human stories.

Most of our caregiving narratives are not so dramatic as Michel's, but all of us who engage in life review during the last third of life come face to face with the struggle to forgive. It is impossible to go beyond the very early days of childhood without feeling disappointment and hurt, and, if we have lived long, we have many memories of both. Difficulties with family members and friends tend to accumulate over the life span, and interpersonal problems multiply. Both minor disappointments and major difficulties add up. They challenge our ability to forgive others, ourselves, and God.

However, this accumulation is no cause for despair, for the passing of years can also bring increased opportunities for personal contemplation, leading to wisdom. In some people, like Michel, these reflections result in increased empathy for others (in her case, for victims of abuse), broader perspectives, and deeper humility. Although serious hurts can remain so poignant that an older adult speaks of an incident that took place many years ago as though it had just happened yesterday, these wounds do not inevitably lead to endless ruminating and a sense of victimhood. Forgiving, resilient elders find that they can "re-story" their lives,[10] trust in God's promises, and begin to cling to hope.

Perhaps because it impacts our past, present, and future so profoundly, forgiveness calls forth the strongest and most complex human emotions we endure. Nevertheless, the process of forgiveness becomes highly important to us during the last third of life, when time and energy are limited.[11] Gerontologists have theorized that, when time is running out, adults are more likely to give priority to emotional goals, rather than to knowledge-related goals, as in the younger years.[12] Thus, for elders, there may be a desire to forgive because of the positive feelings it creates. Or, they may make efforts to avoid unforgiveness because it is such a painful burden.

As Michel's story reveals, forgiveness is complicated, messy, and painful. Although after minor relational problems, forgiving can be quick and easy (more like overlooking), when there have been deep violations of trust, as in sexual abuse, the process can take years of effort and prayer. There are even times, I believe, when talking about forgiveness may not be helpful. When accompanying persons like Michel, I find myself speaking of *healing* or *laying down a burden*. What is important is not our terminology but healing that allows the victim of extreme hurt to move on with her life.

Michel's story teaches much about forgiveness, including what it is not. It is important to identify misunderstandings of forgiveness, since they can harm people who are moving on a forgiveness journey.

What Forgiveness Is Not, at Any Age

Personal experiences, combined with my research and clinical work, have convinced me that many common myths about forgiveness are simply wrong. Forgiveness, for example, does not mean condoning or excusing harmful acts. After grave hurts such as Michel's, it is both hurtful and morally wrong to imply that forgiveness is a get-out-of-jail-free card. God gave us the Law as well as the Gospel, the gift of justice as well as mercy. To condone an evil act, or to insist that forgiveness be prematurely granted, cheapens suffering and is insulting beyond words to a victim.

Neither does forgiveness remove all pain from human memories, nor take us back in time to the person we were before. Michel will, no doubt, shed tears about her father off and on throughout her life, as she continues to grieve the many losses he caused those she loves. She will continue to think back to the trip she made to confront him, when he confessed but made a very weak, self-centered

Forgiving, resilient elders find that they can "re-story" their lives, trust in God's promises, and begin to cling to hope.

apology. She described that painful day to me as a kind of loss of innocence, as a moment when she changed her perceptions of not only her father but of the entire world.

Michel also taught me to refute another myth, that forgiveness requires an apology. It certainly makes forgiveness easier when an apology is given, but hearing "I'm sorry" falls into the category of desirable but not necessary. Michel's father most likely had a narcissistic personality disorder, and he was never able to empathize with those he hurt or realize the family damage he had caused. Nevertheless, she chose not to wait impotently for him to understand or respond. She decided that his indifference would not hold her in bondage, year after year.

Perhaps the most important myth to refute, however, is that forgiveness and reconciliation always occur together. This is a dangerous myth and has often been used, for example, by nominally Christian men or women who abuse their partners. But anyone who has been deeply wounded needs to be reassured that it is neither wise nor spiritual to deliberately place oneself in harm's way. The best a victim can hope for in dealing with a physically or verbally violent perpetrator is to seek safety and stay away. This is one of the reasons I supported Michel's decision to not become her father's personal caregiver. Her safety would not be certain. Restored relationships are typically impossible in situations of extreme harm, such as murder or sexual abuse.

Forgiveness and Letting Go

Resiliency is often more noticeable in people who have suffered dramatic harm, like Michel. But there are many stories that are less visible, particularly in our domestic lives. For example, Alice too can find a quiet path to resiliency, if, with God's help, she can gradually leave her resentment for Harry's drinking behind. In both cases, in situations of either ordinary or extraordinary injury, forgiveness is a crucial part of continuing strength.

> Anyone who has been deeply wounded needs to be reassured that it is neither wise nor spiritual to deliberately place oneself in harm's way.

It makes intuitive sense that spiritually resilient people would also be forgiving people. But being resilient, or spiritually resilient, does not mean that forgiveness comes easily or cheaply. Many speak of it as a painful journey, or find a different metaphor to describe what they are going through as victims. At first, victims may feel separated not only from other people but also from God, and ask many *why* questions. Then, as time passes, the resilient begin to create more complex and nuanced narratives about their experiences of harm. For Michel, this meant recognizing that not all men were abusers or adulterers. She was motivated to change the plot of her story because she wanted peace and love in her life, and anger stood in her way. But getting there was not a smooth trajectory; some days she felt calm, but on others the rage and pain returned.

Michel shared a moment in her forgiveness process that has stayed with me and become a resource in my writing, teaching, and spiritual life. One day, about ten years after she began struggling to forgive her father, she was standing in church, singing the words of the liturgy, "Lord have mercy, Christ have mercy, Lord have mercy." Thinking suddenly of her father, she began to pray silently, "I can't do anything more with this man, Lord. He's all yours. I give him to you." She told me that she experienced a sense of peace and calm at the end of the service that has not left her. "It was almost like an exorcism," she told me. This spiritual experience helped her to move on, and for her, it was enough. Michel envisioned her father, from that time on, as God's responsibility. She believes that his sins are part of the burden Christ carried to the cross, along with the pain of his victims. For Michel, that was enough.

Understanding how people react to harm, and how some persons choose to inflict harm on others, is a never-ending challenge. Every time I attempt to understand another human being, let alone myself, I rediscover that becoming wise, like the practice of forgiveness, is a lifelong process. Even now, I cannot fully know what Michel was going through, and I can only partially imagine how Alice and Harry's story will end.

The Beauty of Forgiveness

Some days, when I feel discouraged by human brokenness, especially a heavy story such as Michel's, I use music or some other form of art to remind myself that we live in a beautiful world. In my home office, I have hung a large canvas reproduction of Rembrandt's *Return of the Prodigal Son*. This painting inspired pastoral-care scholar Henri Nouwen to write a book about the parable, and it inspires me to experience God's welcome and try to forgive.

I believe that forgiveness is not only a moment of peace and wisdom. It is a thing of beauty. Consider, for example, the moment when the welcoming father embraces his prodigal son (Luke 15:11–32). This embrace has not only caught the imagination of artists like Rembrandt through the centuries, but countless people have been moved to tears as they have watched and heard the story of the father and son's embrace. Dramatists, writers, musicians, and other visual artists have interpreted this parable as a story of repentance and return, passionate embrace, and the re-forming of desire. The embrace of loving father and repentant son is a vision of re-membering and reunion. Suddenly and mostly unconsciously, we sense the profound elegance central not only to our own experience but to all of created and redeemed reality—the elegance at the heart of the world. We gaze at the father and have a glimpse of the love of God. We look at the broken son and see ourselves.

Forgiveness is a journey to beauty but not necessarily one of romance (although some artistic renditions of the prodigal son have been highly romantic). Just as the forgiveness work that Alice, Michel, and all of us have to do is hard, untidy, and imperfect, so is that work also beautiful, in the same way the face of the dying Christ on the cross is beautiful. When we become forgivers, we somehow participate in the beauty that is at the heart of the universe, a beauty that creates and redeems us because it can do no other.

> Forgiveness is not only a moment of peace and wisdom. It is a thing of beauty.

Unforgiveness, on the other hand, is ugly and horrific. Unforgiveness is something we would rather not gaze upon or hear about; something makes us turn away and ignore. This story is not sentimental. The prodigal son does not sit romantically in some café, mulling over his estrangement. He feeds the pigs; he is splattered with their excrement. He picks up, no doubt, horrific illnesses of body and mind. His road home is not a hero's path, either, as in some fantasy tale or Greek myth. He walks, he struggles, he almost perishes; he faces mundane troubles that threaten to undo him. Like the overly romanticized moment when death comes to our human bodies, unforgiveness is stinky and grotesque. It is Auschwitz and Rwanda, not Paris in spring time.

But when forgiveness occurs, when the embrace between loving Father and repentant child happens, we see more than the splendor of a father's love—more, even, than our own forgiveness by a loved one, human or divine. What we witness is beyond human attachment because it points outside each individual to all that exists—to the glory of any forgiveness story ever told. We see, we intuit, in the moment of forgiveness, a place of love, safety, and understanding. We believe again in life as a meaningful enterprise and trust again in its promise. We are beautiful, washed clean, and vibrant because we are redeemed, brought home, and set free.

Reflection on Psalm 51:1–12

Have mercy on me, O God,
according to your steadfast love;
According to your abundant mercy,
blot out my transgressions
Wash me thoroughly from my iniquity,
and cleanse me from my sin.
For I know my transgressions,
and my sin is ever before me.
Against you, you alone, have I sinned,
and done what is evil in your sight,
So that you are justified in your sentence,
and blameless when you pass judgment.
Indeed, I was born guilty,
a sinner when my mother conceived me.
You desire truth in the inward being;
therefore teach me wisdom in my secret heart,
Purge me with hyssop, and I shall be clean;
Wash me, and I shall be whiter than snow,
Let me hear joy and gladness;
let the bones that you have crushed rejoice.
Hide your face from my sins,
and blot out all my iniquities.
Create in me a clean heart, O God,
and put a new and right spirit within me.
Do not cast me away from your presence,
and do not take your holy spirit from me.
Restore to me the joy of your salvation,
and sustain in me a willing spirit.

PSALM 51 is a cry for forgiveness. "Blot out my transgressions! . . . Cleanse me from my sin," David calls. Since his encounter with the prophet Nathan (2 Samuel 12), the king has been pondering his sin ("my sin is ever before me") and now, after hearing the parable Nathan told him, he finally "gets it." He recognizes himself in the story and sees himself for what he is. David is ready to accept the judgment against him, Nathan's pointed accusation, "You are the man." As he writes this psalm, he no longer focuses on political or military power, no longer is obsessed with having any sexual partner he desires. His only hope now is that God will not cast him out forever as he deserves. All he wants is a restored, joyous reunion with his God.

To understand the background for this psalm, we must read 2 Samuel 12, but we know the psalm was written after David's vision of himself drastically changed. He moved from a false view of himself and his glory in the world to one of repentance, humility, and a desire for truth. Before Nathan confronted him, David thought of himself as all-powerful, as someone who could do whatever he wanted, simply because he could. "Whatever he wanted" included stealing a general's wife and murdering the general. But this mighty king was actually a prisoner in his own story. The words of a brave prophet were needed to break the bonds that David created for himself—and Nathan's pronouncement did indeed free him.

Over the centuries since this psalm was composed, people of faith have prayed, "Create in me a clean hear, O Lord." When I was young, we sang it together every Sunday as the offering was presented. David's sin was quite dramatic—certainly more interesting than most of our mundane transgressions. But because all our sins cast us away from God's presence, they are important and worthy of being pondered. The psalm is so popular precisely because we resonate with David's situation, even in our own little worlds of pettiness, irritability, and greed.

David's story teaches us that forgiveness, including accepting God's forgiveness, means overcoming a wide range of barriers. These include pride, fear, resentment, and hopelessness. Sitting alone and pondering our sins will not do it. We must also take responsibility for them, admit that we should be judged, and then beg for mercy. Why? Not so that we have the illusion of outward righteousness restored, like a political figure standing before a crowd and "confessing" after he is exposed in the press. Rather, we confess and beg God's forgiveness so that we can be brought back into a loving, close relationship with God. At any age, in any situation, we need to be set free from the bonds that destroy the joy of life. We need to confess and be forgiven.

I believe that before we can ever ask for forgiveness ourselves, much less forgive our enemies, we must have a heart-to-heart conversation with God, as David did. We must own up to who we really are; we must repent. This owning up includes honestly considering our negative emotions—the dark parts of our moods and the greed, jealousy, and anger we feel. We also need to take another look at our position in the world. Are we quite so glorious and admired as we imagine, or would we be if others saw us the way God does? We need this uncomfortable self-knowledge to become wise. As David recognized, self-knowledge does not mean becoming wise in the eyes of the world, where whoever has the most toys wins, but wise in our secret hearts, where we most need clear vision (not merely in the eyes of the world).

During the stress of caregiving, there are many times we are not at our best. Both our actions and our secret thoughts are not anything we'd like to publish. Yet, God sees and knows them all and waits patiently for us, hoping we will return to his love, to a joyous reunion with him. God is the prodigal son's father—watching out for our return and hoping we can join in the community's work for God's realm after our return. All this reunion requires is a secret conversation—a heartfelt prayer of repentance and a cry for forgiveness. All it takes is that we fess up to who we are and tell God

At any age, in any situation, we need to be set free from the bonds that destroy the joy of life. We need to confess and be forgiven.

how much we want to experience the renewal and peace that only God's forgiveness can bring.

I sometimes think of the strange words about sin that were said over me, and are said over us all, at baptism: "In baptism, our gracious heavenly Father frees us from sin and death by joining us to the death and resurrection of our Lord Jesus Christ."[1] This is a reminder that repentance is a first step, but we have been freed from the bonds of sin through someone else's sacrifice. Jesus is the reason we can rest at night, assured that no matter what we have done or said, we are forgiven. We need forgiveness not only for the personal peace it brings but so that we can get up the next morning and get back to work.

The work we do on behalf of God's world, including personal or professional caregiving, is not so dramatic as the vast plans God had for David, but each of us has important tasks to do each day. This has been God's plan for us all along, lifelong. At our baptism, we heard that the Holy Spirit would be sent into our lives, and we can count on this no matter how mundane we think the ministry we have is. I think of Bonnie and her prayers for God's help as she quietly cared for so many people with dementia through the years. I think of Sam and Sally and their devotion, and of Elenore and her determination to join her mother on the dementia journey. All of these servants of God lived into Christian life—repentance, renewal, and spirited service.

The Christian life—and forgiveness itself—is, in the end, not an individual matter alone. As a community we need to confess, be renewed, and get to work—together. Throughout this book there are thoughts about how congregations can become more significant in the lives of caregivers and those with dementia. But spiritual communities, too, get off track, sin, and need divine forgiveness. They need to break out of the bonds that hold them back and to hear the truth, including the truth of false priorities and human pride. Only then can we join each other in humble service—the service of the forgiven, the service of those in whom God has created clean hearts.

6

Reality Is a Cloud of Possibilities: Grace and Creativity

MARY IS tired. It has been a long day—one that began with a struggle over bathing and dressing and went downhill from there. Now it is lunch time, and Mary calls a friend and reports that she is already exhausted. Does she have the energy to get through the rest of the day, she wonders? Is there any way to feel renewed and refreshed?

The experience of caring 24/7 for someone with dementia includes urgent demands that become part of daily existence. The long hours, the constant need for decisions about level of care, the difficult physical and emotional work—these experiences impact a caregiver greatly and can make someone like Mary think that she has no choices. But what if there are hidden emotional, social, and spiritual opportunities, even within Mary's daily reality, including surprising possibilities for creativity and joy? And what if these possibilities could actually renew her energy?

As a former caregiver myself, I would never disagree with the truth that caregivers must live with many things we cannot change. But I also believe that there are important exceptions. We can shape numerous aspects of our lives so that we remain open to moments of connectedness with other people, with the universe. We can plan ways to experience, with our care partner, pleasurable, imaginative activities. We can use the resources we already have at hand— imagination, courage, and the expertise of others—to break out of what can seem like an inflexible, gloomy life. Unclear as these possibilities may appear, especially on a hard day, believing that they are possible is the first step toward increasing grace and joy in our lives. Best of all, believing in fresh opportunities can make it far easier to live with that uninvited guest, dementia.

A Cloud of Possibilities

Cognitive psychologist Amos Tversky wrote, "Reality is not a point; it is a cloud of possibilities."[1] As he did so, he changed "how we think about how we think."[2] Along with his lifelong research partner, Daniel Kahneman, Tversky researched how we make decisions, a topic with exciting implications for everything from business to sports to the social sciences. What Tversky and Kahneman found was that we do not decide what to do on the basis of rationality alone. Rather, much of what we decide is not predictable based on either past experiences or statistical analysis. These departures from perfect rationality can even be anticipated, the psychologists found.

I am interested in Tversky and Kahneman's ideas because they have implications for dementia and caregiving. We know that perfect rationality is no longer possible with serious cognitive impairments. Is there an opening here for seeing life with dementia not only as less predictable but also as a creative adventure? Caregivers, professional and personal, constantly make decisions about what persons with dementia are capable of, and we do so from our point of view, from our understanding of reality. These decisions may seem perfectly rational to us, yet they may neglect a cloud of possibilities. Perhaps we need to rethink how we think about dementia. Perhaps we need to think more imaginatively about the creative self.

Prominent psychologist Mihaly Csikszentmihalyi has created his own definition of creativity—one that goes beyond the limited definition in the *Oxford Dictionary*, "Creativity: The use of imagination or original ideas to create something. Inventiveness."[3] Csikszentmihalyi implies that when we are creative, we not only use our imaginations to be inventive. We participate in the goodness

> Perhaps we need to rethink how we think about dementia. Perhaps we need to think more imaginatively about the creative self.

of life. Creativity then becomes a model for living that includes positive goals and excitement.

What does all of this have to do with living with dementia? What exactly is a creative way of life for a caregiver and their care partner? Sometimes we understand a term best by looking at its opposite. Let me present two contrasting visions from my experience as a nursing home chaplain. These brief visions—which are a summary of actual experiences—provide pictures of both the absence and presence of creativity.

In the first vision, it is one hour before lunch time. To save time, the nursing assistants have already wheeled people, all of whom are living with dementia, up to the nurses' station in their reclining wheelchairs. Now, and for the next sixty minutes, they will sit and wait for lunch. Some have fallen asleep, one man is trying to get out of his chair, and one woman is yelling, "I want to go home!" The only other sound in the hallway is the voice of a nurse talking on her cell phone. The walls are bare of any art work, except for a child's drawing inside the station, out of view of the patients. This scene is repeated every day, seven times a week.

In a different facility, it is also one hour before lunch, but the atmosphere is very different. Classical music is playing softly (although tomorrow it might be jazz or soft rock). The hallways in this facility are brightly decorated with a combination of work by the residents themselves and reprints of classical art that were chosen by the residents (those by impressionists seem to be most popular). The residents here also have dementia, but they are down the hall in the craft room where the activity director and several volunteers from the community are encouraging them to finish a project.

Today these residents are making supplies for a game they will play tomorrow. They are using the color samples from a paint store, attaching them to clothespins that they have painted to match. Each person gets to choose a color, and some decide to decorate the paint chips that are left over. It is clearly important that they finish, because they have been promised that their work will be used in a matching game tomorrow.[4] One of the women remarks that she likes the wooden clothespins better than "those plastic ones that break." Another person comments that his favorite color is purple. Although several of the residents need help, no one is asleep, and most seem engaged and interested

Where would you rather live? That is obviously a rhetorical question! The total lack of sensory stimulation in the former facility is, sadly, common in some long-term care locations I have known. Residents have few or no goals, they have difficulty even staying awake (although I realize they may also be medicated), and life seems meaningless for long hours each day. In the second facility, there is excitement and joy. The residents have a goal, they are making decisions and are engaged in a simple but meaningful craft. They are also surrounded by the beauty of visual arts and by music. They are no longer passively waiting for something to happen or someone to come. They are participating in the goodness of life.

Not surprisingly, persons with dementia who have opportunities to participate in creative activities have more energy, are easier to manage, require less medication, and are more likely to connect to others.[5] For these reasons alone, residential facilities need to improve and increase activities and environments. They need to believe in that cloud of possibilities! But is this only a fantasy? Can people living with dementia actually participate in creative activities? Ironically, persons living with dementia are sometimes more imaginative and flexible than those of us who are caregivers. And they are certainly more ready to live in the present moment.

One person with early Alzheimer's disease put it this way, "Please understand that after the diagnosis, we have time to plan and live life to the fullest. Each day is a gift. Is that any different from how anyone should strive to live his or her life?"[6] He reminds us that each day is a gift regardless of our cognitive abilities. We caregivers are also freed to be in the present when we move away from our regrets about the past and fears for the future. We join those we love who are living with dementia and are already there, waiting for us!

> Not surprisingly, persons with dementia who have opportunities to participate in creative activities have more energy, are easier to manage, require less medication, and are more likely to connect to others.

What could be more important than to leave our anxieties behind for a time, and suddenly to truly be there—not under the cloud of dementia, but under the cloud of possibilities.

Everyone, not only artists and composers, has received the gift of imagination. Caring for someone with an impaired memory or the loss of verbal skills can make us aware of this gift in fresh and exciting ways. There are many paths to discover this gift. At times, it arises out of moments shared by care partners (the person living with dementia and their caregiver) or with extended family. Other times, creativity emerges outside the home as part of simple activities at church or during community events. Sometimes unexpected grace moments show up when we are simply sitting silently with the person we love and care for. Finally, at perhaps the most meaningful times of all, these moments occur when no one plans them, when they simply happen, surprising us with their beauty.

We all hunger for beauty, whether we can articulate this need or not. One of the most prevalent misunderstandings of imaginative experiences for all older adults, including those with dementia, is that the arts are simply another way to entertain. This leads to false ideas (too often put into practice in senior programming) that older adults hate modern art, that they don't want to be disturbed by anything beyond their comfort zone, or that they don't need to be genuinely involved in what they do. My research and writing with gerontologist Susan McFadden suggests that older adults are open to imaginative moments when they can experience encounters with something beyond themselves, something "numinous."[7]

Two of the examples we described in an article on this subject are (1) getting together in a church basement to engage in simple crafts (most persons with early dementia can participate at this level), and (2) visiting an art museum (see the documentary *Almost Home*).[8] There are so many ways to encounter beauty. Why not attend a Beethoven symphony or a country music festival (tastes vary!), or accompany a person with dementia on a nature walk to collect

> Older adults are open to imaginative moments when they can experience encounters with something beyond themselves, something "numinous."

fall leaves? These are only a few of the ways that the boredom of dementia and caregiving can be exchanged for an encounter with aesthetic aspects of life. It is difficult to observe a person deeply engaged with the arts or other creative activities and then justify the environments in many institutions, such as the facility I describe above.

Imaginative Moments through Worship

While creativity is an important aspect of caregiving relationships, it is even more central to our worship. Several years ago, I had the opportunity to interview four of my colleagues at Luther Seminary who had for many years been preaching and leading worship for vulnerable elders, many of whom had impaired memories, in a long-term care facility in St. Anthony Park Home in Saint Paul, Minnesota. They were delighted to share their impressions and experiences with me, and they told me of their own personal reactions to caregiving and aging. I was particularly struck with my colleagues' ability to combine their active, creative love for these residents with sound biblical theory—namely, their conviction that people of any age are created in God's image (and thus deserve respect) and have important roles to play in God's kingdom.

My colleagues did not find planning to lead worship for persons with dementia to be either obvious or easy. The apparent lack of response from the nonverbal folks was especially challenging, but rather than withdrawing or simply going through the service routinely, they worked hard to break through, to find those moments that mattered. "They want to hear the gospel, and they light up when they do," New Testament scholar Roy Harrisville commented.

All four of these volunteer preachers spoke of how important worship moments beyond the sermon were for those persons living with dementia. The familiar words of the Lord's Prayer, well-known hymns, Holy Communion—these were the vehicles for the work of the Spirit in the here and now. Wendell Fredrichs, professor emeritus of Old Testament, spoke of a woman who could no longer sing, "She would beam during the singing. She was singing in her heart and mind, even without her voice." What a lovely insight into the spirituality of those who can no longer tell us how much they need and love God.

If we truly believe that our spiritual journeys do not end when dementia shows up, if we understand the deep need for spiritual community that is present at any stage in life, if we trust that there is a cloud of possibilities for our worship time together, then why not think of how our worship might be more creative to better enable spiritual connections for those with dementia. As one of the pastors I interviewed for this book said, these special people can continue to participate in the liturgy, pray the Lord's Prayer, and join in the Apostles' Creed—and who knows what spiritual power these experiences work in their hearts.

Those of us who are congregational leaders need to consider how dementia-friendly our Sunday experiences actually are. Persons living with dementia attend our worship services every week—or fail to do so because we have not planned adequately to welcome them. What kind of music do you include in worship each week? While it is interesting to learn new contemporary liturgies and hymns, the more traditional and familiar music touches most of the senior members, including those with dementia. Are there opportunities to greet people at worship who have impaired memories, and is that done in such a way that they are not embarrassed by forgetting names? What about after the service? Do social gatherings include opportunities for persons with dementia and their caregivers to be welcomed and to interact with other members? If the answer to these questions is no, it may be time to begin with some educational programs that will assist your congregation in understanding both persons living with dementia and their spiritual needs.

There is a power at work in our lives that goes beyond human imagination, and worship is one of the places where that power

If we truly believe that our spiritual journeys do not end when dementia shows up, . . . then why not think of how our worship might be more creative to better enable spiritual connections for those with dementia.

breaks in. The stories my colleagues told me were a reminder that there is so much going on in spiritual communities and that worship is one way that faith and beauty can enter the lives of the most vulnerable among us. I was moved by the devotion of my colleagues and came to appreciate them on a deeper level after listening to them. I later wrote of what I learned from the interviews: "Something unique happens when the Word is heard in hymns, linked to musical memories long gone from the conscious mind—an entirely different part of the human brain responds."[9]

I was happy to share these stories in an article because I believe that stories, such as my colleagues' narratives of quiet service in a nursing home, belong to and create communities. There are so many loud stories of selfishness, violence, and greed around us that it is sometimes difficult to hear the stories of grace in our communities. Because we are called to work for the kingdom of God in any way we can, we have, I am convinced, an obligation to share narratives about loving caregivers—like my colleagues, and like the caregivers I interviewed for this book. As I consider these moments, I add: "Now to him who by the power at work within us is able to accomplish abundantly far more than all we can ask or imagine, to him be glory" (Eph 3:20).

Now to him who by the power at work within us is able to accomplish abundantly far more than all we can ask or imagine, to him be glory.

Creative Experiences in the Family

The visions I shared early in this chapter of two different care facilities highlight a difference between connections and accompaniment. But what about persons living at home, with caregivers or in their own homes or cottages? What might creativity have to do with accompaniments there?

The scenes of persons living with dementia in private homes also vary greatly. Some folks with dementia spend most of the day in front of a TV. They have little sensory stimulation and no reason to stay awake. Others are engaged in creative activities (see suggestions below) and live in an environment that is rich and colorful. Most are somewhere in the middle, but caregivers may need to be reminded of the cloud of possibilities, the need to diversify daily experiences. As suggested earlier, these can include everything from activities with the fine arts to simple crafts.

But just who is going to plan and organize these activities? Is this just one more way to make tired caregivers feel guilty if they don't also plan for arts and crafts? You may be surprised to learn that when care partners find ways to participate in activities together, both feel more energetic and less depressed. And you certainly don't have to do the activities alone. If there are no other caregivers around, find out what is going on your community, through organizations such as the Alzheimer's Association, or at a local day care center. Even better, call the grandchildren and invite them over to help! Perhaps you have asked yourself, "How can I get my children or my grandchildren, grandnieces, or grandnephews more involved with my mother?" Simple activities provide opportunities for all ages in a family to enjoy being in the moment and to be there together! The only requirement is the ability to be playful so that you can improvise when you need to.

I began taking my children with me to work on special occasions when I served as chaplain in a long-term care facility. Other times, I would bring a resident home to have dinner with us. Watching my children, I made an important discovery: young people are often better than adults at relating to older adults, including those with memory loss. Young people are less bound by preconceived ideas of what to do and say, and they have an easier time staying in the moment. If you leave behind the idea that it is not appropriate to involve children as members of your caregiving team, if you decide that they might bring in new ways to have fun and lighten everyone's day, they will eagerly take on this important role. They will also provide some of the hugging and touch that persons with dementia sorely need and receive some extra attention themselves in the midst of a busy day.

Children are especially valuable if, for example, the adult caregiver is having a bad day and being impatient with their care partner.

That's a good time to try turning over the conversation to a younger person in the family. You may be surprised by what happens next. Even when a grandmother no longer remembers her grandchildren's names, she will light up and respond with a smile to their simple and direct words.

Dementia-Friendly Activities

But what to do when we get together? Favorite hobbies, things the person with memory loss has always enjoyed, are the best place to start. They can be modified and reinvented to adjust for capacities today. Did Grandfather like to go fishing? Why not bring him some lures and ask for his advice on which fish they are used for. Or perhaps Grandma loved to sing. You can begin informal sing-alongs and make a personal playlist (on an iPad, iPhone, or other streaming device). Music can also get us moving. People with memory loss typically love to move to music. Depending on the physical ability of your care partner, you can also turn on your video and do your regular workout, inviting your parent or spouse—and your children as well if they are present—to join in.

Other activities are similar to what older adults have always enjoyed doing with children. Again, they simply need modification and flexibility. My granddaughter is in kindergarten and learning to read. I sometimes have more opportunities than her busy parents to let her read me a story, over and over. Children visiting or living with a grandparent with memory loss can still practice reading, or work on a simple puzzle, or make those first attempts to play a musical instrument. Of course, looking at photos and photo albums together is another activity loved across the generations. Just don't worry if the memory-impaired person can't recall names.[10] Since the goal is to be creative and playful, content is less important than the ways that children can teach us how to relax, relate, and get lost in the moment.

Young people are often better than adults at relating to older adults, including those with memory loss.

Activities for Care Partners

Of course, not all activities involve children. Care partners themselves often make up their own ways to be flexible and creative. One of the professional caregivers I interviewed, a physician, smiled as she told me about two of her patients. Now in their nineties, they are obviously still crazy about each other. But the husband has developed memory loss, and they have had to discontinue the traveling and dining out they have always enjoyed. His wife told the doctor how they now design their special evenings at home instead. They put on music and dance to the same tunes they loved when they were dating. They both enjoy these moments together—even though the husband is unlikely to remember them tomorrow. This couple was an inspiration to the doctor, who has suggested similar ways to connect to other patients living with dementia.

Painting and other visual-arts activities are fun for most people, even those of us who have little apparent talent in drawing. Looking at art in books or in museums, using paints and markers, coloring in basic coloring books, helping someone weave or create a collage— all of these can inspire care partners to express, create, and connect.

Daily tasks can also provide imaginative and meaningful times together. I spend a great deal of time cooking with my grandchildren these days, and should I develop dementia in my old age (I'm only seventy-two now!), I hope they will invite me to cook with them. Even with dementia, people can do some of the same tasks children do when learning to cook—stirring, breaking the eggs, mixing the batter. And then everyone can enjoy eating the results together!

For others, household tasks are a creative outlet, including gardening, growing indoor plants, or caring for pets. There are few limits when trying to find meaningful and enjoyable activities, so long as they are modified for whatever cognitive and physical abilities the care partner is experiencing. Even people who can no longer walk can participate in activities while seated. The important thing is to begin with something that interests or could interest them, and to be together, sharing "enchanted moments."[11]

Imaginative Moments in Community Groups

Of course, the Holy Spirit's power is not confined to churches or even homes. In community settings, too, there are exciting ways in which imagination is improving the experiences of both living with dementia and caring for someone with dementia. I share just of few of them here, but encourage all caregivers to design what works in their setting.

Gerontologist and psychologist Susan McFadden and her husband, retired pastoral caregiver John McFadden, have worked many years to build dementia-friendly environments. In a recent book, they argue for what they describe as "aging together" in dementia-friendly communities. They use the image of genuine friendship to address dementia and its challenge—an image compatible with my own, since it emphasizes joining with rather than caring for.[12]

The McFaddens' passion for creating a new culture for dementia care also takes tangible forms, particularly in the memory cafés they have founded and supported. Susan[13] and John work across the country to inspire others to begin their own community cafés. These cafés are creative and playful places where early stage persons and their caregivers can be both welcomed and supported. The gatherings are informal, and the settings vary by location, but the hospitality and relaxed nature of the conversation is consistent. Support comes indirectly as people simply hang out and talk to each other in a group where everyone gets it about living with dementia. "I really don't know what we would have done without the memory cafés; I think we would have been confined to our house," commented one participant.[14]

Momentia

Fortunately, not only academics and chaplains are beginning community programs hospitable to persons experiencing dementia and their caregivers. One inspiring example of the latter is the Momentia Group in Seattle. The stated goal of this group is "empowering persons with memory loss and their loved ones to remain connected and active in the community."[15] This very successful and well-known group organizes events, including garden walks, provides a variety of café experiences similar to the McFaddens' memory cafés, and sponsors other activities focused on topics relevant to caregivers and to persons with dementia. They provide links on their website (see the resources at the end of the book).[16] I believe the Seattle program is successful because it never focuses on persons as problems defined by their illness. Planning begins with the person, not the distressed symptoms of their lives (as with the medical model).

Living in the Moment

Welcoming the Spirit into our lives does not always mean that we engage only in organized activities, be it in care facilities, at home, or in the larger community. At times we can simply sit in silence with our loved one and find we are participating in holy moments—holy in that they are unique gifts of the Spirit, not interruptions to our precious plans.

Whether or not we are currently caregivers, modern life is filled with more and more distractions. As technology advances, the potential to expose ourselves to information also increases—at a ridiculously fast speed. What all this distraction is doing to us and to generations to come is worrisome to many of us who still think taking a hike in the woods or attending a symphony is among life's greatest pleasures—and ones that don't need to be instantly described on Facebook to have meaning!

One of the benefits of becoming a caregiver for someone with dementia is that it forces us to slow down, turn everything off, and be quiet. As we sit with the person we love, we can truly listen—to the world around us, to softly spoken words from our care partner, and to God. I have been struck by the frequent mention,

At times we can simply sit in silence with our loved one and find we are participating in holy moments.

in books about dementia caring, of the power of enjoying the present moment (see the caregivers' books in Resources). Whether written by personal or professional caregivers, many persons who care for a loved one describe how recognizing and planning times that are not dependent on memories of the past or the ability to forecast the future became so important to both the caregiver and their care partner. They also describe how simply going with what is happening now can transform the experience of living with dementia

I have not often shared my most valued experience of sitting in silence—perhaps for fear that if I told someone, they would not recognize how precious it was to me. On one of my last visits to Pennsylvania to visit my mother, who had vascular dementia, I was given a remarkable gift. My mother had not spoken for many months—to me, my brother and sister, or her professional caregivers. We were sitting outdoors on a warm spring day, and I told her a few pieces of family news, but mostly we just sat together quietly. I don't remember what I was thinking at that moment, but I know I was sad because my mother could no longer inquire about my children or even tell me how she was feeling. Then suddenly, she lifted her head, smiled at me, and said quietly, "You are a good person."

My mother died several weeks later, surrounded by all her children, but she never spoke again. In keeping with her gracious personality, she had given me a blessing. That was her final gift to me, a grace-filled encounter that confirmed what I've long believed: that the Spirit will enter any room where there is a welcome. It is up to us slow down, open up, and provide the time and space for creative winds to blow.

Reflection on Psalm 34:1–8

I will bless the Lord at all times;
his praise shall continually be in my mouth.
My soul makes its boast in the Lord;
let the humble hear and be glad.
O magnify the Lord with me,
and let us exalt his name together.
I sought the Lord, and he answered me,
and delivered me from all my fears.
Look to him, and be radiant,
as your faces shall never be ashamed.
This poor soul cried, and was heard by the Lord,
and was saved from every trouble.
The angel of the Lord encamps
around those who fear him, and delivers them.
O taste and see that the Lord is good;
happy are those who take refuge in him.

PSALM 34 is one of many psalms of praise in our Bible, and it contains a lovely phrase that reminds us of the Holy Eucharist: "taste and see that the Lord is good." The psalmist is obviously filled with joy and can't help breaking out with a song to express his gladness. He has had such powerful experiences with God that he feels absolutely radiant. Now he not only sings a song of joy and gratitude, but he invites the entire congregation to join in: "let us exalt his name together." He wants all those who are faithful to God to hear. He wants not only his own face but the faces of others to be radiant with joy.

When the power of God breaks into our lives, it sometimes feels like a relief, but mostly it feels like an amazing blessing. We are moved—motivated to express feelings that make us sparkle with happiness. We can't help ourselves—we simply have to sing God's praises.

Artists often report a similar experience in their autobiographies—the need to share what they create. When a moment of beauty occurs, it is not fulfilling for them until they share it with others. They want to engage with others who share their perspective and receive feedback that will inspire them and help them grow creatively. Sometimes, you can tell that an artist is sharing something simply because he is having so much fun with the beautiful sounds and sights he creates that he can't bear to keep them to himself. Can you imagine someone like da Vinci creating his beautiful paintings and then putting them in a closet? Creation is a community affair.

The impulse to ask others to participate in the creative moment is very strong. My twelve-year-old grandson Oliver has an artistic gift, and he is eager to share what he creates. Even though he has only been playing the piano for three years, he constantly surprises us all with the beauty he produces—moving up and down the keyboard, seldom needing sheet music. He understands that this is a gift he has been given by God, and he is currently working on a piece to play at his sister's baptism. When I first suggested that he think about playing on that occasion, he said, "I would really like to do that, to play in church for Nina." For Oliver, music and faith come together seamlessly. What a delight to see!

Not all of us have such gifts (I took piano lessons for nine years and never got very far), but we all can remember moments when, like the psalmist, we know that God was very near. We saw God's goodness; we felt that it was so close we could taste it. Reading Psalm 34 is a reminder that, like moments of creativity, times of powerful faith need to be shared.

I close this last reflection by thanking you, my reader, for permitting me to share some personal moments in this book. I hope that you

We can't help ourselves—we simply have to sing God's praises.

too have had times, as you read, when you could almost taste God's goodness. Perhaps that occurred during the most mundane of days, when it was least expected.

I have such respect and gratitude for what you do, for the love you share with a special person who needs your help. I know that my own perspective has widened as I've listened to some of you tell your stories about living with dementia, and as I've imaged listening to many others. Your vocations are precious to all of us in the church and beyond. God bless, and don't forget that your faces, too, are radiant.

Afterword

Tough Hope

DEMENTIA, INCLUDING Alzheimer's disease, is a terrible illness, and I am praying for a cure. What we need is a cure now; what we all want is a dementia-free world. Five million people in the United States are suffering from Alzheimer's disease alone, and many more face other forms of dementia. These are our parents, spouses, friends, and neighbors. It is unacceptable to watch more and more people each year struggle with this illness. Many of us are motivated to give money, participate in walkathons, advocate for more federal research money, and join organizations that do all of these—because we want a cure, and we want it now!

A cure will not come in a single moment, however. Dr. Keith Fargo, director of scientific programs and outreach at the Alzheimer's Association, believes progress is picking up, but that no one can accurately predict the date for a cure. He writes: "It may be that it won't be one major breakthrough, it'll be a lot of more modest breakthroughs and the eventual treatment will consist of several different approaches, each of which has a modest effect."[1]

Some newly diagnosed men and women participate in clinical trials in order to give meaning to their suffering and to help future generations avoid the ravages of dementia. This is a tremendously important contribution, because the scarcity of volunteers is a huge problem for dementia research. Needed are not only people with early signs of dementia but people who do not currently have memory problems. These clinical-trial volunteers are real hope-givers, practicing love for future generations.

Meanwhile, what do we hope for? If there is hope today for those with dementia and their caregivers, it is not easy, soft, or quick. Slowly we accept the hard truth—our hope for the people we care for today cannot be hope for a medical cure alone.

Dealing with dementia is not for the fainthearted. We have often heard the phrase *tough love*, but I believe we also need tough hope. We need to find hope that acknowledges the terrifying landscape of dementia and the daily challenges of tests, doctors' visits, medications, and constant decline. Only then can we catch glimpses of a different kind of dream, a dream of tough hope—hope that we will have redemptive moments in our lives now, and hope beyond our earthly life, based on the promises of God.

It is sometimes helpful to make a distinction between optimism and hope. These two words may be second cousins, but if so they are cousins once removed. Optimism refers to a specific outcome. One of my own (selfish) forms of optimism is for a cure for degenerative arthritis in the near future. Hope, on the other hand, has a more general focus. I can say I hope to do meaningful work in my life. In working with distressed clients and in pastoring people with urgent problems, I found that hope, not optimism, is the antidote to despair, even as we have to let go of dreams for the specific outcomes we desire, like a cure for a disease. In the face of great suffering, we need tough hope—but it would not make sense to speak of tough optimism.

Hope Now

My friend Jenny cried off and on while I talked to her by phone, but she laughed a little, too. She lives on the opposite coast from me, in California, and I called her recently because I wanted to hear her thoughts on caring for someone with dementia. I knew that Jenny, her sister, Mary, and her father, Bob, had been caregivers for her mother for over nine years as Alzheimer's disease played itself out. For the last five of those years, Jenny's mother was cared for as well by the wonderful staff of a local long-term care facility. But Jenny's

> We have often heard the phrase *tough love*, but I believe we also need tough hope.

father spent long hours each day with his wife, and either Jenny or her sister was always there to feed their mother the evening meal.

Jenny had lots of stories to tell about the family's experience, but what was most interesting were her reports about how giving care had healed the family dynamics and brought Jenny, Mary, and Bob closer together. I knew that Jenny and her sister had been having relationship problems for years, originating in political and religious disagreements that spilled over into judgmental attitudes. Mary practiced a very conservative form of Christianity and appeared to look down on Jenny for many of the choices Jenny made—at least that is how Jenny experienced the relationship. My friend had a history of problems with her father as well—although they were mostly under the surface. Preoccupied and distant, Bob had never given Jenny the affirmation and affection she craved. This lead to difficulties with father figures in other aspects of Jenny's life.

But Jenny said, "Jan, you would be surprised—we really were a team!" My friend described to me how the demands of planning for her mother's care, and being present with her mother faithfully, brought the family into a level of intimacy and affection that had been missing. They needed to be in touch regularly to make plans, so it was impossible for family members to avoid each other. And as they witnessed the tender love and care that others in the care team were providing, new respect and love for each other became possible. After Jenny's mother died, the family dynamics remained close and respectful—never perfect, but healed enough to make everyone glad.

Jenny was now mourning not only her mother's death but her father's as well; he died just a year after her mother. "I'm so glad we had that time together, when my father and I were taking care of my mother," she told me. "I can't tell you how important those years were."

One form of tough hope for family members coping with dementia care is that they will become closer to each other and learn to be more forgiving and loving. This does not always occur, of course.

Some families have the opposite experience—tensions increase and people become more resentful and distant. But if dignity and grace are present, including respect and forgiveness, we can hope for a kind of redemptive suffering, right in the middle of our grief. Healed families are one possibility for tough hope.

Another hope is for increased resiliency. This is more likely when an entire community is there to support a caregiver. Tough hope is especially at home in spiritual community. I discovered this when I interviewed older Germans and Americans for my books on spiritual resiliency.[2] They told me over and over how vital the support of their community was to their ability to cope and thrive during times of crisis (including war and illness). For these older people, hope was a posture that sustained them as many relationships changed and as they came to terms with their ambiguous pasts. Hope gave them not only solace but also the power to go on.

But community care is not consistently provided when it is needed for those with dementia and their caregivers. People typically are supportive when there is a sudden crisis, like the diagnosis of serious cancer or a death in the family. Unfortunately, dementia is an illness that usually lasts for many years, and the simple length of the disease can diffuse a community's desire to bring casseroles, provide respite and visits, and simply call and inquire how things are going. But tough hope thrives on love that is communal. This is a very real challenge for congregations—to remember the importance of accompanying those making the dementia journey, no matter how long it may take. If nothing else, we can make regular calls and visits for those giving care and their partners, bearing in mind the hope we give caregivers and those with impaired memories when we tell them that they are being held in community prayer.

Hope beyond Hope

We also promise individual prayers to those who are hurting. "I'll be keeping you in my prayers." These words often sound more like a polite comment than a genuine promise. But if someone who offers

Healed families are one possibility for tough hope.

Tough hope is especially at home in spiritual community.

to pray also asks, "What would you like me to pray for you?" the prayers become more personal and meaningful. What do we ask for, though? What do we ask a friend, pastor, or community leader to pray for, on our behalf? We can ask for a cure, but we know that is unlikely to come soon. Let's pray fervently for one anyway! So long as we are patient, that is a most appropriate prayer, even when we are no longer optimistic about a quick medical solution.

We could ask for happiness. Time passes slowly when we give care to those with dementia, and there is plenty of time to look back and remember episodes of deep unhappiness. As we age, we notice a pattern of gains and losses in our lives, but we do not always see a neat balance of periods that were happy and those that were sad. Do we pray that we will have a better balance—more days of happiness in the days to come? I think that is a fine prayer. God is ready to hear about anything we need, so we don't need to worry about getting it just right.

Ironically, hope—especially tough hope, as I am labeling it here—increases more frequently in times of suffering and unhappiness than in times of peace and comfort. I discovered this repeatedly when I listened to older adults who were spiritually resilient. They had all been through some of the worst events that can happen to people—a world war that tore apart their country, the loss of loved ones including young children, health problems, and living with chronic pain. But these older adults were the most hopeful people I've ever met. They knew they had suffered and might suffer again, but they had developed tough hope.

Spiritually resilient people learn to rely on God, not on themselves and not even exclusively on the medical community (even though researchers, doctors and nurses are surely God's servants). They have learned to trust in the promises in Scripture, words they heard all their lives, including assurances that they are not alone. Above all, they trust that good things are promised for all God's children.

We Christians are sometimes embarrassed to speak of our final hope, our hope in eternal life. We know that eternal life is not pie in the

> This is a very real challenge for congregations— to remember the importance of accompanying those making the dementia journey, no matter how long it may take.

sky and that it begins in this lifetime as we work for God's kingdom on earth. But Christians also have a hope beyond hope; we have the gift of everlasting life through Jesus's death and resurrection. That is the promise we cling to and are grateful for. That too can be the focus of our prayers when we give up hopes for a quick cure.

As a nursing-home chaplain, I did far too many funerals, but when I tell friends that I'd rather preside at a funeral than at a wedding, I get strange looks. What I mean is that leading a funeral, I can bring comfort to hurting people, and they actually listen to the gospel. In the Lutheran funeral service, we pray, "Acknowledge, we humbly beseech you, a sheep of your own fold, a lamb of your own flock, a sinner of your own redeeming."[3] There is deep, spiritual hope available here, one that often moves me to tears. There is something powerful about hoping that those we love will someday participate, with us, in the mystery of eternal life that God has promised.

Religious denominations today are sharply divided over interpretations of many aspects of biblical theology. Some have a very literal belief in the details about what we will find in heaven (we will all be wearing white robes), and some are so up-to-the-minute that they sound more secular than spiritual (heaven is only what we make of our lives now). In such a climate, hope beyond hope may be difficult to grasp, let alone talk about. Personally, I don't think we need details about either our robes or what heaven will look like, because we have the promises, and these promises are about more than our lives now. They are assurances given by the same God in Christ who made us, entered into human history to redeem us, and rose again so that death would not have the last word. Trusting God's promise—that's good enough for me. That is the only knowledge I need to carry with me into my last days.

We end our exploration of dementia and caregiving with one of the most powerful words of promise in Scripture—words tough enough to give us hope, at any time and in any situation.

> No, in all these things we are more than conquerors through him
> who loved us. For I am convinced that neither death, nor life,
> nor angels, nor rulers, nor things present nor things to come, nor
> powers, nor height, nor depth, nor anything else in all creation, will
> be able to separate us from the love of God in Christ Jesus our Lord.
> (Rom 8:37–39)

I would like to rewrite this just a bit—"neither death, nor life, nor dementia . . ."—because there is no way that dementia is going to get the last word or separate us from God's love. Not only do we have dignity and grace, we are more than conquerors through him who loved us.

Resources: Where Do I Find More Help?

Online Resources

AgingCare.com

- This interactive website provides families with information and support to care for their loved ones. This page is focused on ideas for involving children in dementia care: https://tinyurl .com/ycjzxd9x.

Alzheimer's Association (alz.org)

- The Alzheimer's Association is a well-known, largely voluntary health organization focused on Alzheimer's care, as well as on support and research. Often their information is helpful for other forms of dementia. This page is intended for long-distance caregivers and is appropriate for both early cognitive impairment and mid-stage dementia: https://tinyurl.com /y95z99e7.
- Also by the Alzheimer's Association, this report is a big help in learning the language of dementia: https://tinyurl.com /yde3nwc6.
- National Alzheimer's Café Alliance: For help with finding or starting a memory café in your own community, go to: https:// tinyurl.com/yc7n2tak.

Dementia Emergency (dementiaemergency.com)

- This website was developed in Britain and offers a wealth of information on dementia, including general advice and what to do in medical emergencies. It is free and easy to use.

Elder Care Online (ec-online.net)

- This website offers information on many aspects of caring for older adults. On this page, social worker Jan Allen provides more information on using validation approaches to communicate with persons with dementia and to manage difficult behaviors: https://tinyurl.com/yahfd6hp.

HelpGuide.org

- This online resource is dedicated to a young woman who committed suicide because she lacked resources to deal with her depression. It offers a variety of free materials on various mental-health issues. This page tells you, step by step, how to learn a relaxation exercise very similar to an exercise many counselors use in their practice: https://tinyurl.com/yasyljxo.

Livability.org.uk

- Two organizations in the United Kingdom, Livability and the Alzheimer's Society, have formed a partnership to provide caregiving resources. On this page, they share a pamphlet on developing dementia-friendly congregations: https://tinyurl .com/y8yjyj8f.

Memory Café Catalyst (memorycafecatalyst.org)

- Memory Café Catalyst is an online community connecting people interested in memory cafés (also called Alzheimer's cafés)—community-building gatherings for people experiencing memory loss and their caregivers. They provide links to a variety of dementia-related resources and to people with an interest in memory cafés, along with the latest news about these gatherings.

Momentia (momentiaseattle.org)

- Momentia is a grassroots movement in Seattle, Washington, that seeks to empower persons with memory loss and their loved ones to remain connected and active in the community. This page tells of their "friendly folk-dancing" program, but there are many others: https://tinyurl.com/yaw8lxma.

United States National Library of Medicine, National Institutes of Health (nlm.nih.gov)

- This website has helpful information about many health issues. On this page, the focus is on the prevalence of Alzheimer's disease in the United States: https://tinyurl.com/y8e2h6l3.

Books on Dementia and Caregiving

Boss, Pauline. *Loving Someone Who Has Dementia: How to Find Hope while Coping with Stress and Grief*. San Francisco: Jossey-Bass, 2011.

Brackey, Jolene. *Creating Moments of Joy along the Alzheimer's Journey: A Guide for Families and Caregivers*. Lafayette, IN: Purdue University Press, 2017.

McFadden, Susan H., and John T. McFadden. *Aging Together: Dementia, Friendship and Flourishing Communities*. Baltimore: Johns Hopkins University Press, 2011.

Power, G. Allen. *Dementia beyond Disease: Enhancing Well-Being*. Baltimore: Health Professions, 2014.

Shouse, Deborah. *Connecting in the Land of Dementia: Creative Activities to Explore Together*. Las Vegas, NV: Central Recovery Press, 2016.

Smith, B., and Dan Gasby. *Before I Forget: Love, Hope, Help, and Acceptance in Our Fight against Alzheimer's*. New York: Harmony, 2016.

Thibault, Jane Marie, and Richard L. Morgan. *No Act of Love Is Ever Wasted: The Spirituality of Caring for Persons with Dementia*. Nashville, TN: Upper Rooms Books, 2009.

Glossary

The definitions of the following terms, used in this book, reflect the author's understanding.

Ageism: A way of thinking and acting, based on false beliefs, that ascribes worth to a person based on their age alone.

Alzheimer's disease: One common form of dementia that causes problems with memory, thinking, and behavior. Symptoms usually develop slowly and get worse over time, becoming severe enough to interfere with daily tasks.

Dementia: A major neurocognitive disorder that leads to a decline in mental ability severe enough to interfere with independence and daily life.

Dignity: A sense of being worthy and honored not for one's accomplishments alone but in relationship with God and other persons.

Forgiveness: The process (often lengthy) of moving from passive suffering of victimhood to the active suffering of moving on.

Grace: A complete way to be in the world that reflects appreciation for beauty, love, and forgiveness. Graceful living is a response to the love and forgiveness first given us by God.

Intersubjective space: The social and psychological space between persons in which both are subjects (persons with agency) and neither are objects (treated as means to an end).

Life story: A way to understand human experience and the interpretation of that experience with coherence and meaning. Each person's evolving story is a key component of their individuality.

Mild cognitive impairment: A brain-impairment syndrome that involves the onset and evolution of cognitive problems beyond those expected based on the age and education of the individual but is not severe enough to be classified as dementia. MCI may be a transitional stage between normal aging and dementia.

Narrative: An approach to understanding human actions and motivations based on the settings, characters, plots, and themes we create for our lives. (Many of these are below our conscious awareness.)

Plot breakers: Events that disrupt our plans for the future (our future stories).

Respect: A pattern of relating to another human being that enhances their dignity.

Roles: A part (such as an actor plays) or function assumed and played by a person in a particular situation, as determined by the largely unconscious plot they have created for their life story.

Validation: Entering and reflecting the emotional world of the other person, rather than attempting to change their way of thinking and feeling.

Vascular dementia: A form of dementia caused by problems in the supply of blood to the brain, typically a series of minor strokes. These episodes lead to a worsening ability to think that occurs by noticeable steps, rather than gradually, as with Alzheimer's disease.

Notes

Part One: Introduction

1. Mandy Aftel, *The Story of Your Life: Becoming the Author of Your Experience* (New York: Simon & Schuster, 1996).
2. Paul B. Baltes and Margret M. Baltes, "Psychological Perspectives on Successful Aging: The Model of Selective Optimization with Compensation," in *Successful Aging: Perspectives from the Behavioral Sciences*, ed. Paul B. Baltes and Margret M. Baltes (New York: Cambridge University Press, 1990), 11–34.
3. G. Allen Power, *Dementia beyond Disease: Enhancing Well-Being* (Baltimore: Health Professions, 2014), loc. 193, Kindle.
4. Peter V. Rabin and Nancy L Mace, *The 36-Hour Day: A Family Guide to Caring for People Who Have Alzheimer Disease, Related Dementias, and Memory Loss*, 5th ed. (Baltimore: Johns Hopkins University Press, 2011).
5. Janet L. Ramsey, "Caring at a Distance: A Need for Spiritual Resiliency," Chicago Chaplain's Network's *The Link*, 2003, 7–10.
6. I believe strongly that we need to advocate politically so unpaid caregiving workers receive adequate compensation and are recognized as part of what a civil society appreciates from its members.
7. One recent example is a book by David Brady, *Serenity: Aging with Dignity, Living with Grace* (New York: Post Hill Press, 2016).

Chapter 1: What I Want Most Is Respect: Dignity and Life with Dementia

1. Jackie Robinson, *I Never Had It Made: An Autobiography of Jackie Robinson* (New York: HarperCollins, 2013), 294.
2. Wikipedia, s.v. "Dignity," last updated December 9, 2017, https://tinyurl.com/y9l37rr9.

3. Jessica Benjamin, *Shadow of the Other: Intersubjectivity and Gender in Psychoanalysis* (New York: Routledge, 1998).

4. Martin Luther, *Luther's Small Catechism with Explanations* (St. Louis, MO: Concordia, 2008), 21.

5. Richard Taylor, *Alzheimer's from the Inside Out* (Baltimore: Health Professions, 2007).

6. Richard Taylor, foreword to *Dementia beyond Disease: Enhancing Well-Being*, by G. Allen Power (Baltimore: Health Professions, 2014), loc. 106, Kindle.

7. For more information on caregivers' health challenges, see Alzheimer's Association, "Alzheimer's Disease Caregivers," *FactSheet*, March 2017, https://tinyurl.com/yc6eepn9.

8. Janet Ramsey and Rosemary Blieszner, *Spiritual Resiliency and Aging: Hope, Relationality, and the Creative Self* (Amityville, NY: Baywood, 2013).

9. This is true in America but not in all places of the world. In some cultures, a nature cycle of generational care exists that leads to completely different attitudes about dependency. See further, "7 Cultures that Celebrate Aging and Respect Their Elders," *Huffington Post*, last updated May 18, 2015, https://tinyurl.com/y9rl6vfq.

10. Unfortunately, I am unable to locate the original source for this story.

11. Oscar Tranvåg, Oddgeir Synnes, and Wilfred McSherry, eds., *Stories of Dignity within Healthcare: Research, Narrative, and Theory* (London: M&K Publishing, 2016).

Reflection on Psalm 23

1. Janet Ramsey and Rosemary Blieszner, *Spiritual Resiliency and Aging: Hope, Relationality, and the Creative Self* (Amityville, NY: Baywood, 2013), 27.

Chapter 2: I Learned to Join in the Journey: Dignity as Accompaniment

1. Kathryn Witta, retired executive director of Covenant Care Communities (personal communications with author, 2017).

2. Annie Parsons and Claire Hooker, "Dignity and Narrative Medicine," *Journal of Bioethical Inquiry* 7, no. 4 (2010): 345–51.

3. Luciana Cramer, "Savvy Caregiver: Thou Shalt Not Argue," in Alzheimer's Association California Central Coast Chapter's *Caregiver Tips and Tools* 10 (2016): https://tinyurl.com/y7d6usc7.

4. Albert Mehrabian, *Silent Messages: Implicit Communication of Emotions and Attitudes* (Belmont, CA: Wadsworth, 1972).

5. Mark D. Tranvik, *Martin Luther and the Called Life* (Minneapolis: Fortress Press, 2016).

6. Tranvik, *Martin Luther*, 97.

Reflection on Psalm 38:9–22

1. Frederick J. Gaiser, *Healing in the Bible: Theological Insight for Christian Ministry* (Grand Rapids: Baker Academic, 2010), 83.

2. "Gladys Wilson and Naomi Feil," YouTube video, 5:46, uploaded by "MemoryBridge," May 26, 2009, https://tinyurl.com/lzojdng.

Chapter 3: I Know These People Mean Well: Dignity and Congregations

1. Dietrich Bonhoeffer, *The Cost of Discipleship* (New York: Macmillan, 1963).

2. Janet L. Ramsey and Rosemary Blieszner, *Spiritual Resiliency and Aging: Hope, Relationality, and the Creative Self* (Amityville, NY: Baywood, 2013), 156.

3. Ramsey and Blieszner, *Spiritual Resiliency and Aging*, 157.

4. Joseph Jebelli, *In Pursuit of Memory* (London: John Murray, 2017).

5. Robert N. Butler, *Why Survive? Being Old in America* (Baltimore: Johns Hopkins University Press, 2002).

6. See further the work of developmental psychologist Robert Kegan, *In Over Our Heads: The Mental Demands of Modern Life* (Cambridge, MA: Harvard University Press, 1998).

7. Thomas Reynolds, *Vulnerable Communion: A Theology of Disability and Hospitality* (Grand Rapids: Brazos, 2008).

8. Judith V. Jordan, *Women's Growth in Connection: Writings from the Stone Center* (New York: Guilford, 1991), 82.

9. *Book of Common: Prayer and Administration of the Sacraments and Other Rites and Ceremonies of the Church* (New York: Church Publishing Incorporated, 1979), 305.

10. *Book of Common Prayer*, 308.

Part Two: Introduction

1. For a more complete definition of grace, see *Merriam-Webster's Collegiate Dictionary* (online), s.v. "grace," https://tinyurl.com /y9xrndgf.

2. Lois Malcom and Janet Ramsey, "On Forgiveness and Healing: Narrative Therapy and the Gospel Story," *Word and World* 30, no. 1 (Winter 2010): 23–32.

Chapter 4: What's Love Got to Do with It?
Grace and Love

1. David Robson, "There Really Are 50 Eskimo Words for 'Snow,'" *Washington Post*, January 14, 2013, https://tinyurl.com/yczchmvn.

2. See further, Merriam–Webster Word Central Student Dictionary, s.v. "love," https://tinyurl.com/y9s79mcg.

3. David Wolpe, "We Are Defining Love the Wrong Way," *Time*, February 16, 2016, https://tinyurl.com/y9j8hswm.

4. Jim Steinman, writer and composer, "Making Love Out of Nothing at All," audio, track 6 on Air Supply, *Greatest Hits*, Warner/Chappell Music, 1983.

5. Sridharan Ramaratnam, "Leprosy Neuropathy," Medscape, October 9, 2017, https://tinyurl.com/yatxfldf.

6. I have adapted the phrase "good enough caregiver" from Winnicott, who described a "good enough parent." D. W. Winnicott, "The Theory of the Parent-Infant Relationship," *International Journal of Psycho-Analysis* 41 (1960): 585–95.

7. Susan H. McFadden and John T. McFadden, "The Role of Congregations in Dementia-Friendly Communities," *Caring Connections* 11, no. 3 (2014): https://tinyurl.com/y9xuew99.

8. Sonya Laputz, "Personality Changes in Dementia," in Alzheimer's Association, California Central Chapter's *Caregiver Tips and Tools* 30, https://tinyurl.com/y75l36m7.

9. Laputz, "Personality Changes in Dementia."

10. Michael White, *Maps of Narrative Practice* (New York: W. W. Norton, 2007), 24.

11. "Intimacy, Sexuality and Alzheimer's Disease," Alzheimer's Association, July 2014, https://tinyurl.com/y7lm9vdx.

12. Tara Parker-Pope, "Seized by Alzheimer's, Then Love," *New York Times*, November 14, 2007, https://tinyurl.com/ya96stz3.

13. Cynthia Ramnarace, "Till Dementia Do Us Part?," AARP, September 13, 2010, https://tinyurl.com/y8gcl752.

Reflection on Psalm 107:1–9, 43

1 Rolf A Jacobson and Karl N. Jacobson, *Invitation to the Psalms: A Reader's Guide for Discovery and Engagement* (Grand Rapids: Baker Academic, 2013), 153.

Chapter 5: If Only . . . : Grace and Forgiveness

1. To listen to Rabbi Weiman-Kelman on the topic of forgiveness in interreligious understanding, go to "Week Five: Forgiveness in the Middle East," in "Season for Interfaith-Intercultural Celebration: 9-Week Self Study Program," Association for Global Thought, https://tinyurl.com/ybzdft4t.
2. See further, Solomon Schimmel, *Wounds Not Healed by Time: The Power of Repentance and Forgiveness* (New York: Oxford University Press, 2002).
3. Emily903, "Islam: Teachings on Forgiveness and Reconciliation" (diagram), GetRevising, April 26, 2016, https://tinyurl.com /y7u3v5tu.
4. See further, Integrated Research Institute, "A Review of *Christianity and Genocide in Rwanda*," Université Chrétienne Bilingue du Congo, March 2, 2016, https://tinyurl.com/y7kzgszs.
5. "Amish Grace and Forgiveness," *Lancaster PA Blog*, https://tinyurl .com/yc32sfgr.
6. Mark Berman, "'I Forgive You.' Relatives of Charleston Church Victims Address Dylann Roof," *Washington Post*, June 19, 2015, https://tinyurl.com/y8eadxsu.
7. Lewis B. Smedes, *The Art of Forgiving* (New York: Ballantine, 1996).
8. See, for example, Lois Malcolm and Janet Ramsey, "On Forgiveness and Healing: Narrative Therapy and the Gospel Story," *Word and World* 30, no. 1 (Winter 2010): 23–32.
9. Martin Luther, *Luther's Works*, vol. 26, ed. Jaroslav Pelikan (St. Louis: Concordia Publishing House, 1963), 284.
10. Dan P. McAdams, *The Stories We Live By: Personal Myths and the Making of the Self* (New York: Guilford, 1993).

11. Sheung-Tak Cheng and Ying-Kit Yim, "Age Differences in Forgiveness: The Role of Future Time Perspective," *Psychology and Aging* 23, no. 3 (2008): 676–80.
12. Laura L. Carstensen, Derek M. Isaacowitz, and Susan T. Charles, "Taking Time Seriously: A Theory of Socioemotional Selectivity," *American Psychologist* 54, no. 3 (1999): 165–81.

Reflection on Psalm 51:1–12

1. *Evangelical Lutheran Worship* (Minneapolis: Augsburg Fortress, 2006), 227.

Chapter 6: Reality Is a Cloud of Possibilities: Grace and Creativity

1. Quoted in Michael Lewis, *The Undoing Project* (New York: W. W. Norton, 2017), 313.
2. Cass R. Sunstein and Richard Thaler, "The Two Friends Who Changed How We Think about How We Think," *The New Yorker*, December 7, 2016, https://tinyurl.com/y8s3wwo8.
3. *Oxford Living English Dictionaries*, s.v. "creativity," https://tinyurl.com/ybrfwppx.
4. For more on this project, see "Explore Nursing Home Activities and More!," Pinterest, https://tinyurl.com/yblhpvo6.
5. Deborah Shouse *Connecting in the Land of Dementia: Creative Activities to Explore Together* (Las Vegas, NV: Century Recovery Press, 2016).
6. Oak Knoll Lutheran Church and Lyngblomsten, *If We Forget . . . : Wisdom and Reflections from Those Living with Memory Loss* (Saint Paul, MN: CreateSpace, 2012).
7. Susan H. McFadden and Janet L Ramsey, "Encountering the Numinous: Relationality, the Arts, and Religion in Later Life," in *A Guide to Humanistic Studies in Aging: What Does It Mean to Grow Old?*, ed. Thomas R. Cole, Ruth E. Ray, and Robert Kastenbaum (Baltimore: Johns Hopkins University Press, 2010), 163.
8. McFadden and Ramsey, "Encountering the Numinous," 172–73.
9. Janet L. Ramsey, "Love, Call, and Coming Home: Preaching the Word to the Very Old," *Word and World* 33, no. 1 (2013): 89.

10. For great ideas on activities with children, see Leonard J. Hansen, "An Addition to Your Caregiving Team: Your Parent's Grandchildren," AgingCare.com, https://tinyurl.com/ycjzxd9x.

11. Jolene Brackey, *Creating Moments of Joy along the Alzheimer's Journey*, 5th ed. (West Lafayette, IN: Purdue University Press, 2017), loc. 208, Kindle.

12. Susan H. McFadden and John T. McFadden. "The Role of Congregations in Dementia-Friendly Communities," *Caring Connections* 11, no. 3 (2014): https://tinyurl.com/y9xuew99.

13. Susan is research and development consultant for the Fox Valley Memory Project in Wisconsin.

14. Gloria Siebers, quoted by Alison Dirr, "Cafes Celebrate Five Years of Helping Those with Memory Loss, Their Caregivers," *Post-Crescent*, November 9, 2017, https://tinyurl.com/y8kr4m9d.

15. See Momentia's website at www.momentiaseattle.org.

16. "Momentia Partners," Momentia, https://tinyurl.com/y8kxsmst.

Afterword: Tough Hope

1. R. Sam Barclay, "Alzheimer's Disease: What Stands Between Us and a Cure?," *Healthline Newsletter*, July 31, 2015. https://tinyurl.com/yap6460s.

2. Janet Ramsey and Rosemary Blieszner, *Spiritual Resiliency and Aging: Hope, Relationality, and the Creative Self* (Amityville, NY: Baywood, 2013); Janet L. Ramsey and Rosemary Blieszner, *Spiritual Resiliency in Older Women: Models of Strength for Challenges through the Life Span* (Thousand Oaks, CA: Sage, 1999).

3. *Evangelical Lutheran Worship* (Minneapolis: Augsburg Fortress, 2006), 283.

Bibliography

Aftel, Mandy. *The Story of Your Life: Becoming the Author of Your Experience.* New York: Simon & Schuster, 1996.

Alzheimer's Association. "Alzheimer's Disease Caregivers." *FactSheet,* March 2017. https://tinyurl.com/yc6eepn9.

"Amish Grace and Forgiveness." *Lancaster PA Blog.* https://tinyurl.com/yc32sfgr.

Baltes, Paul B., and Margret M. Baltes. "Psychological Perspectives on Successful Aging: The Model of Selective Optimization with Compensation." In *Successful Aging: Perspectives from the Behavioral Sciences,* edited by Paul B. Baltes and Margret M. Baltes, 1–34. New York: Cambridge University Press, 1990.

Barclay, R. Sam. "Alzheimer's Disease: What Stands Between Us and a Cure?" *Healthline Newsletter,* July 31, 2015. https://tinyurl.com/yap646os.

Benjamin, Jessica. *Shadow of the Other: Intersubjectivity and Gender in Psychoanalysis.* New York: Routledge, 1998.

Berman, Mark. "'I Forgive You.' Relatives of Charleston Church Victims Address Dylann Roof." *Washington Post,* June 19, 2015. https://tinyurl.com/y8eadxsu.

Bonhoeffer, Dietrich. *The Cost of Discipleship.* New York: Macmillan, 1963.

Book of Common: Prayer and Administration of the Sacraments and Other Rites and Ceremonies of the Church. New York: Church Publishing Incorporated. 1979.

Brackey, Jolene. *Creating Moments of Joy along the Alzheimer's Journey.* 5th ed. West Lafayette, IN: Purdue University Press, 2017. Kindle.

Buber, Martin. *I and Thou.* New York: Simon & Schuster, 1970.

Butler, Robert N. *Why Survive? Being Old in America.* Baltimore: Johns Hopkins University Press, 2002.

Carstensen, Laura L., Derek M. Isaacowitz, and Susan T. Charles. "Taking Time Seriously: A Theory of Socioemotional Selectivity." *American Psychologist* 54, no. 3 (1999): 165–81.

Cheng, Sheung-Tak, and Ying-Kit Yim. "Age Differences in Forgiveness: The Role of Future Time Perspective." *Psychology and Aging* 23, no. 3 (2008): 676–80.

Cramer, Luciana. "Savvy Caregiver: Thou Shalt Not Argue." In Alzheimer's Association California Central Coast Chapter's *Caregiver Tips and Tools* 10 (2016): https://tinyurl.com/y7d6usc7.

Csikszentmihalyi, Mihaly. *Creativity: Flow and the Psychology of Discovery and Invention.* New York: HarperCollins E-books, 2007.

Dirr, Alison. "Cafes Celebrate Five Years of Helping Those with Memory Loss, Their Caregivers." *Post-Crescent,* November 9, 2017. https://tinyurl.com/y8kr4m9d.

Evangelical Lutheran Worship. Minneapolis: Augsburg Fortress, 2006.

Gaiser, Frederick J. *Healing in the Bible: Theological Insight for Christian Ministry.* Grand Rapids: Baker Academic, 2010.

"Gladys Wilson and Naomi Feil." YouTube video. 5:46. Uploaded by "MemoryBridge," May 26, 2009. https://tinyurl.com/lzojdng.

Hansen, Leonard J. "An Addition to Your Caregiving Team: Your Parent's Grandchildren." AgingCare.com. https://tinyurl.com /ycjzxd9x.

Integrated Research Institute. "A Review of *Christianity and Genocide in Rwanda*." Université Chrétienne Bilingue du Congo, March 2, 2016. https://tinyurl.com/y7kzgszs.

"Intimacy, Sexuality and Alzheimer's Disease." Alzheimer's Association, July 2014. https://tinyurl.com/y7lm9vdx.

Jacobson, Rolf A., and Karl N. Jacobson. *Invitation to the Psalms: A Reader's Guide for Discovery and Engagement*. Grand Rapids: Baker Academic, 2013.

Jebelli, Joseph. *In Pursuit of Memory: The Fight against Alzheimer's*. London: John Murray, 2017.

Judith V. Jordan*, Women's Growth in Connection: Writings from the Stone Center*. New York: Guilford. 1991.

Kegan, Robert. *In Over Our Heads: The Mental Demands of Modern Life*. Cambridge, MA: Harvard University Press, 1998.

Laputz, Sonya. "Personality Changes in Dementia." In Alzheimer's Association, California Central Chapter's *Caregiver Tips and Tools* 30. https://tinyurl.com/y75l36m7.

Lewis, Michael. *The Undoing Project: A Friendship that Changed Our Minds*. New York: W. W. Norton, 2017.

Luther, Martin. *D. Martin Luthers Werke*. Vol. 5. Weimar: H. Böhlau, 1883.

———. *Luther's Small Catechism with Explanations*. St. Louis, MO: Concordia, 2008.

———. *Luther's Works*. Vol. 26. Edited by Jaroslav Pelikan. St. Louis: Concordia Publishing House, 1963.

Malcom, Lois, and Janet Ramsey. "On Forgiveness and Healing: Narrative Therapy and the Gospel Story." *Word and World* 30, no. 1 (Winter 2010): 23–32.

McAdams, Dan P. *The Stories We Live By: Personal Myths and the Making of the Self.* New York: Guildford, 1993.

McFadden, Susan H., and John T. McFadden. "The Role of Congregations in Dementia-Friendly Communities." *Caring Connections* 11, no. 3 (2014): https://tinyurl.com/y9xuew99.

McFadden, Susan H., and Janet L. Ramsey. "Encountering the Numinous: Relationality, the Arts, and Religion in Later Life." In *A Guide to Humanistic Studies in Aging: What Does It Mean to Grow Old?*, edited by Thomas R. Cole, Ruth E. Ray, and Robert Kastenbaum, 163–81. Baltimore: Johns Hopkins University Press, 2010.

Mehrabian, Albert. *Silent Messages: Implicit Communication of Emotions and Attitudes.* Belmont, CA: Wadsworth, 1972.

Oak Knoll Lutheran Church and Lyngblomsten. *If We Forget . . . : Wisdom and Reflections from Those Living with Memory Loss.* Saint Paul, MN: CreateSpace, 2012.

Parker-Pope, Tara. "Seized by Alzheimer's, Then Love." *New York Times*, November 14, 2007. https://tinyurl.com/ya96stz3.

Parsons, Annie, and Claire Hooker. "Dignity and Narrative Medicine." *Journal of Bioethical Inquiry* 7, no. 4 (2010): 345–51.

Power, G. Allen. *Dementia beyond Disease: Enhancing Well-Being.* Baltimore: Health Professions, 2014. Kindle.

Rabin, Peter V., and Nancy L. Mace. *The 36-Hour Day: A Family Guide to Caring for People Who Have Alzheimer Disease, Related Dementias, and Memory Loss.* 5th ed. Baltimore: Johns Hopkins University Press, 2011.

Ramaratnam, Sridharan. "Leprosy Neuropathy." Medscape, October 9, 2017. https://tinyurl.com/yatxfldf.

Ramnarace, Cynthia. "Till Dementia Do Us Part?" AARP, September 13, 2010. https://tinyurl.com/y8gcl752.

Ramsey, Janet L. "Caring at a Distance: A Need for Spiritual Resiliency." Chicago Chaplain's Network's *The Link*, 2003, 7–10.

———. "Love, Call, and Coming Home: Preaching the Word to the Very Old." *Word and World* 33, no. 1 (2013): 82–91.

Ramsey, Janet L., and Rosemary Blieszner. *Spiritual Resiliency and Aging: Hope, Relationality, and the Creative Self.* Amityville, NY: Baywood, 2013.

———. *Spiritual Resiliency in Older Women: Models of Strength for Challenges through the Life Span.* Thousand Oaks, CA: Sage, 1999.

Reynolds, Thomas. *Vulnerable Communion: A Theology of Disability and Hospitality.* Grand Rapids: Brazos, 2008.

Robinson, Jackie. *I Never Had It Made: An Autobiography of Jackie Robinson.* New York: HarperCollins, 2013.

Robson, David. "There Really Are 50 Eskimo Words for 'Snow.'" *Washington Post*, January 14, 2013. https://tinyurl.com /yczchmvn.

Schimmel, Solomon. *Wounds Not Healed by Time: The Power of Repentance and Forgiveness.* New York: Oxford University Press, 2002.

"7 Cultures that Celebrate Aging and Respect Their Elders." *Huffington Post*, last updated May 18, 2015. https://tinyurl.com /y9rl6vfq.

Shouse, Deborah. *Connecting in the Land of Dementia: Creative Activities to Explore Together.* Las Vegas, NV: Century Recovery Press, 2016.

Smedes, Lewis B. *The Art of Forgiving: When You Need to Forgive and Don't Know How.* New York: Ballantine, 1996.

Steinman, Jim, writer and composer. "Making Love Out of Nothing at All." Audio. Track 6 on Air Supply, *Greatest Hits*. Warner/ Chappell Music, 1983.

Sunstein, Cass R., and Richard Thaler. "The Two Friends Who Changed How We Think About How We Think." *The New Yorker*, December 7, 2016. https://tinyurl.com/y8s3ww08.

Taylor, Richard. *Alzheimer's from the Inside Out*. Baltimore: Health Professions, 2007.

———. Foreword to *Dementia beyond Disease: Enhancing Well-Being*, by G. Allen Power. Baltimore: Health Professions, 2014. Kindle.

Tranvåg, Oscar, Oddgeir Synnes, and Wilfred McSherry, eds. *Stories of Dignity within Healthcare: Research, Narratives, and Theories*. London: M&K Publishing, 2016.

Tranvik, Mark D. *Martin Luther and the Called Life*. Minneapolis: Fortress Press, 2016.

White, Michael. *Maps of Narrative Practice*. New York: W. W. Norton, 2007.

Winnicott, D. W. "The Theory of the Parent-Infant Relationship." *International Journal of Psycho-Analysis* 41 (1960): 585–95.

Wolpe, David. "We Are Defining Love the Wrong Way." *Time*, February 16, 2016. https://tinyurl.com/y9j8hswm.